WILDFL

GARDE

WILDFLOWERS FOR EVERY
GARDEN SITUATION

GARDENING with NATURE

Production and Design by:
Webbs Barn Designs
Crib, Dinchope, Craven Arms, Shropshire SY7 9JJ
01588 673019
www.webbsbarn.co.uk

ISBN 0-9541116-3-X

Typeset, Printed and Bound by Arsis Print

Other publications by Jenny Steel:

The Gardening with Nature Series:
Making Meadows
Butterfly Gardening
Wildlife Ponds

Bringing a Garden to Life
Wildflowers for Wildlife

This book is dedicated to Stanley Woodell, tutor and friend for more than 30 years.

Contents

CHAPTER 1
INTRODUCTION

The importance of wildflowers in the countryside

Few of us can have failed to notice radical changes in our countryside over recent years. These are things we read about in our newspapers and hear about on the news, almost on a weekly basis. These changes include many diverse factors especially loss of habitat, removal of hedgerows, building of roads and houses and the implementation of farming practices very different from those employed a hundred or even fifty years ago. However these changes are viewed, either as progress or as backward steps, the results have been that much of our countryside has been radically altered. These changes have seriously depleted the wealth of native wildflowers we once saw around us and our native wildlife has been seriously affected as a result. The decline of many bird species, the loss of bumblebees and lack of butterflies and other insects, have all been linked, rightly or wrongly, to these changes.

How does this relate to our gardens?

Encouraging wildlife into gardens has always been a priority for a minority of people. Over the last twenty years, this way of managing gardens has become much more main stream and now many people would say that to a greater or lesser extent, they consider and make provision for the wildlife in their gardens. In a recent survey, as many as 30% of householders said they fed the birds in their gardens in some way. Many conservation organisations now advocate wildlife gardening as a means of helping to compensate for habitat loss. Figures show that some species, including amphibians such as frogs and toads, rely to a large extent on garden habitats (in this case garden ponds) for their continued survival, as their wild habitats continue to disappear. Wildlife gardening really can make a difference. It is unlikely that rare species are protected from extinction by the enlightened gardeners who welcome wildlife, but it is certain that many species of invertebrates, birds, mammals, amphibians and reptiles can comfortably find shelter and food in our gardens when their requirements are catered for. This means growing the plants that they depend on, and managing our gardens in a way that is sympathetic to the sometimes complicated life cycles of our native creatures. A little knowledge about our native wildlife can go a long way towards helping it.

One very positive and easy thing that we can do to ensure that wildlife visits our gardens, or even takes up residence, is to grow some native wild plants. This includes not just the wildflowers we are talking about here, but also wild trees and shrubs, which are not covered in this book. But how can growing wild plants attract a hedgehog or a frog to a garden? In order to understand this concept we have to take a closer look at the ecology of gardens and the 'food chain' that exists there.

Garden food chain

Every garden, no matter how devoid of vegetation, will contain a large number of invertebrates. This is a group of animals that includes the insects (bees, butterflies, beetles etc.), molluscs (slugs and snails), spiders, earthworms, and several other groups of creature

that we may easily overlook. They will exist in the soil, in or under dead wood, in the compost heap, tucked under almost every leaf of every plant, or they could simply be flying about in the air. These small animals form the backbone upon which virtually all our other garden wildlife depends, either directly or indirectly. They are the focus around which everything else revolves. Invertebrates provide food for just about anything that might visit our gardens, from foxes and badgers (which eat a lot of earthworms), to green woodpeckers (feeding on ants). It is really quite simple: no ants in your garden means that you are unlikely to regularly see a green woodpecker – a gorgeous bird that anyone would be delighted to have visiting their garden.

Wildflowers are an essential part of the garden foodchain: this bumblebee is visiting a foxglove

The importance of these small invertebrate creatures, which are so vital to the garden food chain, cannot be emphasised enough. If we are interested in helping wildlife, our task as gardeners is to encourage as many of these invertebrates as we can to inhabit our plots. If we are successful in that, everything else, over time, follows naturally.

So, how do we get these 'minibeasts' to take up residence? There are many techniques that we can employ, and a general wildlife gardening book (see page 90) will outline these. But the one really important thing we can do is include native plants. Our minibeasts, over time, have evolved to depend upon our native wild plants for food or shelter. They are used to them, they are adapted to the chemicals they contain, they are attracted to their scent. Many of these plant-insect associations are extremely complicated but others are very simple. For example, the small tortoiseshell butterfly will only lay her eggs on a nettle leaf. She knows it by its scent and seeks it out specifically for this purpose – it is the only plant her caterpillars will eat.

This interaction of plants and invertebrates is the natural way of things, and something we can use to our advantage when deciding what to plant in our gardens if we want to attract wildlife.

What is a wildflower?

This is a very important question. For the purposes of this book, a wildflower is a British native plant – a species that has evolved over time alongside our animal wildlife. Without going into great detail about time scales (some plants have been on our shores for much longer than others) the wildflowers described in this book are considered to be native using the New Flora of the British Isles by C. A. Stace (see the Further Reading section on page 90). This therefore excludes some species, for example corncockle, which most people would assume is a native but is an introduced wildflower. It was probably brought to our shores by the Romans, along with crop seeds, long enough ago for it to become an important part of our farmland flora, and then to disappear again! This does not mean that it is not a beautiful addition to a garden or that it is not valuable if you wish to attract wildlife. It simply means that because it is not technically

Many butterfly species, including the small tortoiseshell, love field scabious

7

a British native, it has not been included in the lists of plants that you will find later in this book.

A word here about 'naturalised' wildflowers. These are species that have usually escaped from garden situations to establish themselves in the countryside. Many of these we have happily accepted and plants as familiar as broad-leaved everlasting pea, evening primrose and (probably) snowdrop are all examples. These again are not included in the later chapters of this book. Many naturalised plants are harmless and even a useful addition to our native flora, but others cause huge problems, for instance Himalayan balsam and Japanese knotweed. They may even threaten our own native flora and fauna, so they are omitted from this book.

Another anomaly to mention here is the wildflower in an unfamiliar colour. Colour variation in wildflowers, for example the white foxglove or pink violet, is a relatively common and naturally occurring phenomenon. These are really useful additions to any wildflower garden so you may wish to grow them.

Some books on wildflower gardening include species that are certainly not native, but are suitable for 'wild' gardens or are 'wildflowers' in other countries. The vast majority of the plants we grow in our borders are wildflowers from somewhere else in the world so this can be a confusing and even problematic assumption. These plants are not included in this book.

One very important thing to emphasise at this point is that we are talking about native wildflowers for gardens, not for roadside verges, the grassy banks outside your house, or even a field you may own somewhere. The proliferation in the countryside of non-native species or wildflowers grown from seed that is not native in origin is becoming a huge problem, and something which, as responsible gardeners, we do not wish to make worse. Make sure you are confident that the wildflower you wish to grow really is native, and even then, keep it

The white variety of our native pink foxglove occurs naturally in the countryside

inside your garden boundary. If you stick to the recommended plants in this book, you won't go wrong. If you do have an area that is not strictly 'garden' where you would like to introduce wildflowers, seek the advice of your local Naturalist Trust or the organisation Flora Locale. Contact details for these organisations can be found on page 91.

Where can we grow them?

Having mentioned the idea of not allowing your wildflowers to spill outside your boundaries, we have already introduced an important concept. But with that in mind, there are places in any garden, however small, where wildflowers may be grown. There is a native wildflower for every situation, no matter how dry, wet, shady or hot. Suitable flowers for wet, sunny or shady spots, to grow in grass or containers or for a wild patch are suggested in the different chapters in this book, and six 'star' plants are recommended for each situation. There are also sections on which wildflowers to avoid – not all are suitable for garden cultivation and indeed there are a few that can be highly invasive. These plants have their place in the wider countryside, but are only suitable for the largest garden, if that!

Growing rare wildflowers

Why are some wildflowers rare, whilst others are relatively common? Those that are uncommon generally live in very specialised habitats and for that reason alone are usually difficult to grow in cultivation, even if you are able to find a legitimate source of plant or seed. They may even languish in your garden for a few weeks and then die. For the average gardener, growing plants such as orchids really isn't worth the trouble and if you do see a source of these beautiful plants for sale, they might have been taken illegally from the wild. If you get a chance to go to a nature reserve where rare plants grow, take the opportunity to visit and admire them, and appreciate them in their natural habitat, but don't be tempted to covet them for your garden.

What if you are not interested in attracting wildlife?

The first chapter of this book has assumed that you are interested in growing wildflowers in order to make a good habitat for wildlife in your garden. But of course you may not be interested in attracting wildlife, and perhaps would like to grow these plants only for their beauty and versatility. Many people appreciate the simple elegance of our native flowers, or would like to grow them because they are reminded of their childhood or wild places they have visited. Wildflower gardening is becoming increasingly popular for these important reasons. This book will certainly cater for those interests by showing you how to propagate native flowers and where they can be grown. You may just find that the wildlife-attracting aspects of the flowers you grow and love become ever more important, as you begin to notice the difference that these flowers will make to the web of life in your garden.

CHAPTER 2
HOW TO GROW WILDFLOWERS

Are wildflowers difficult to grow?

There is a general assumption that 'wildflowers' are different from 'garden flowers' in some subtle way which can make them difficult to grow. This is not really the case. All plants require the same basic elements from their environment – a substrate in which to grow, water, nutrients and light. Every plant has its own preferences in terms of the amount of each of these factors it prefers, but of course this applies to all plants – not just our native species. The key to growing wildflowers successfully is to find out which conditions they favour in the wild, and to choose those that prefer the soil type and conditions of light and shade that prevail in your garden. Gardening within your existing conditions, rather than trying to change those conditions to suit the plants you would like to grow, is a sensible rule for any type of gardening. Gardening with nature, rather than against it, is far more likely to produce a successful and harmonious garden than one where you are continually manipulating the environment to produce something that could look unnatural, and not really in harmony with its surroundings. Sadly, many professional show gardens purporting to be 'natural' take the first approach – a tumbling mountain stream with marginal wildflowers looks fabulous in rural Wales, but not perhaps in the heart of a big city. Here, a small copse of birch trees with red campion and bluebells underneath or a lawn with delicate wildflowers would not look out of place.

Wildflowers are particularly suitable for producing an informal, natural-looking garden that sits happily in its surrounding landscape whether that is countryside, city centre or suburbia. The trick is to choose plants that are right for you and your situation.

Obtaining wildflowers

Our native species are far more likely to be found in garden centres or plant nurseries than they were ten years ago. However, there can still be confusion in the plant nursery trade as to whether something is a native or not, or untrained staff might assume that a scabious is a scabious, whether it is actually our native field scabious or a cultivated variety. It may not matter that much to you – perhaps it is just the shape, the colour and the scent that appeal to you and that's absolutely fine. But if you are planning to plant British native wildflowers in your garden it really is worth making sure that you obtain true natives, especially if you are hoping to attract wildlife. Page 91 of this book has a list of plant nurseries and wildlife gardening suppliers, some of them operating a mail order service, where you can obtain native wildflowers of a reliable origin.

However, it is far more exciting (and cost effective) to grow your own plants from seed.

Also you may well find that the range of wildflowers available at your local nursery is rather limited whereas a wide variety of seeds are available. Unfortunately many people, even hardened and competent gardeners, are under the impression that plants are difficult and fiddly to grow from seed. It is true that some wildflowers are notorious when it comes to refusing to germinate, but this is generally because many of them have quite specific germination requirements, and if we don't know what these are at the outset, we are not going to be terribly successful. Once we know what conditions the seeds need and take those into account, the vast majority of native plants are easy and very rewarding to grow from seed. Inevitably you end up with more plants than you can use and the excess can be given to friends, or even sold (properly labelled) for a charity or at a fund-raising event. But of course, don't be tempted to plant your spare seedlings outside your own garden.

Thrift, or sea pink, has pollen for many insects

As responsible gardeners we must be careful about the provenance of our seeds. Don't be seduced by companies that advertise 'mixed wildflowers' or 'seed mats' – these are often not native plants but mixtures of natives and other easy to grow plants such as English marigolds, which are not 'English' at all. 'Wild' in many cases (see Chapter 1) does not mean native and it is important that your seeds are native in origin. Check with the seed supplier if you are in any doubt, and if they are vague about their seed origins, go elsewhere. Good suppliers will make a point somewhere in their catalogue of declaring the origin of all their wildflower seeds and many will supply a certificate to confirm their provenance.

The perils of growing non native

In the past twenty years many seeds of wild plants that occur in the British Isles have been sold and planted, but the seed has been collected from plants growing somewhere in Europe. The species is correct but the plants from which the seed was collected did not grow here. Does this really matter? The answer is definitely 'yes'. The fact that there are close relationships between plants and native animals plays a part here. There is a great deal of variation in the genetic make–up of individual plants within one species, and those native to our country will have a slightly different genetic make-up to those from continental Europe. All the invertebrates associated with those plant species, be they moth caterpillars, bees, slugs or anything else, will be adapted to their local plants and not plants to from Eastern Europe. Many areas in the wider countryside - motorway verges for instance – have been sown with these 'non-British' seeds and the consequences are complicated and potentially damaging to our own native flora and fauna.

Bumblebees are attracted to knapweed for both pollen and nectar

For this reason you may even wish to obtain seeds of wild plants from your own local area if they are available – there will be even more chance of a strong link between the plants and invertebrates that live on them. Your local Wildlife Trust may be able to help you with sourcing local seeds. If you would like to find out more about this subject, and the consequences of not growing native, contact the organisation Flora Locale. Their details can be found on page 91.

So does this mean that it would be sensible to collect the seed of the wildflowers we would like to grow, from the countryside in our own area? Technically yes, but you may, like me, have a problem with this. It is, of course, illegal to collect the seeds of certain rare species and a list of these can be obtained by contacting the Botanical Society of the British Isles (see page 91) or by looking at their website (www.bsbi.org.uk), but it is not illegal at the moment to collect seeds of common plants. If the plant is plentiful or produces millions of seeds (field poppy would be a good example) it would do little harm to collect a few seeds to germinate for garden use, as long as this is done with care and consideration. Once you have even a single plant of a species thriving in your garden, you can happily collect seed from it to increase your own population. There is a good chance it will seed of its own accord anyway. However, even common plants may have seeds that are an important food source for birds or mammals, so I personally never collect wildflower seeds, whether the plant is common or not. I prefer to obtain them from a reputable commercial grower where they have been grown specifically for garden use. This way I know exactly what I am getting and where it originally came from.

Germinating from seed

So let's assume that you have obtained from a specialist grower some wildflower seeds that are guaranteed to be native and have decided to try your luck at germinating them. If you succeed you will be rewarded, generally, with a wealth of seedlings to pot up and plant out in your borders, a garden meadow area or maybe underneath your trees or shrubs. But how do we get to that stage? As has already been mentioned, many wildflower seeds will only germinate under certain conditions, and to give you some help, each of the star species that is recommended in the rest of this book has those conditions indicated. Some species benefit from a little help in order to germinate well. There are two main ways in which we can affect germination.

Stratification (or Vernalisation)

This refers to the practice of reproducing the fluctuating temperatures in which the seeds find themselves in the wild. The majority of seeds fall to the ground in summer and autumn, and lie until the spring before germinating. During the winter weather, changes in temperature break the natural dormancy of the seeds, and germination then occurs when temperatures rise in spring. We can imitate these natural temperature fluctuations by putting our seeds into the fridge or freezer to reproduce winter temperatures. Alternatively we can sow them in the winter months to allow natural conditions to work on them.

Cornfield annuals are easy to grow and wonderfully showy all summer long

Scarification

Some seeds, generally larger ones, have especially tough seed coats. Scarification involves rubbing the seed with fine sandpaper, chipping it in some way or soaking the seeds in warm water to break down the seed coat. These practices speed up the germination process, which in some wildflower species might normally take more than a year. In the wild, this chipping away at the seed coat happens naturally over time by the action of frost and the rubbing of particles of soil against the seeds.

Primrose: one of the delights of spring in a wildflower garden

How to sow

The best way to grow your own wildflowers from seed is to sow them into pots of compost. Sowing them directly where you want them to grow in the garden will work for many annual species such as poppies or cornflowers, but for the perennials or biennials mentioned in later chapters, sowing into pots and then planting them where you want them is by far the most effective way of establishing them. That way they won't get lost or eaten by birds or mice! For the majority of species a small plant pot of maybe 9cm diameter will produce more than enough seedlings for an average garden. Fill your pot with fine textured peat-free compost. You can add an equal quantity of loam if you wish (you can purchase bags of sterilised loam from garden centres) as most wildflowers prefer a compost as much like natural soil as possible. Composts based entirely on coir are sometimes rather lumpy but those that use a mixture of recycled materials generally produce good results. If your compost does appear to be rather coarse, you can sieve out the larger pieces. Don't overfill the pot, and firm it gently. Many professional gardeners have a small flat piece of wood with little handle attached (mine is home made), for firming the compost. If you overfill you will impede the compost drainage, which may result in your seeds failing to germinate. Next sow the seeds thinly on the surface of the compost. The easiest way to do this is to take the packet, cut off the top with scissors and then fold one side to make a sharp crease. Gently tip the packet and allow the seeds to trickle along the crease onto the surface of the compost distributing the seeds as evenly as you can. Don't feel obliged to use them all. It is better to sow a few seeds thinly and reseal your packet for later use. Store your excess seeds somewhere cool and dry and the majority will remain viable for several years.

The seeds must now be covered. This should be done with a gentle touch – many seeds require some light to germinate, and covering them with an inch of soil (a very common mistake) means seedlings are unlikely to ever appear. The easiest way to avoid this problem is to use a fine layer of horticultural grit to cover them, which again is available from garden centres. If the seeds you are sowing are especially small, for example wild marjoram, sow them on top of the layer of grit and they will drop down into the spaces. Light can reach them here and they will not be lost under a thick layer of compost. Water your pots with a fine rose on the watering can, put them in a safe place outside (it is not necessary to use a greenhouse), and don't forget to keep them moist. A little gentle watering if conditions have been dry is all that is needed. Only seeds of plants such as marsh marigold or devil's-bit scabious, which naturally grow in very wet places, need to sit in a saucer of water. Most prefer to drain well between waterings.

Once your seedlings have germinated (and this may take a few days or many weeks, depending on the species) you can pot them up and grow them to a reasonable size before planting them out, or you can prick them out into plant plugs. These 'mini-pots' are especially useful if you are planning to plant your wildflowers in grassy areas.

Timing of sowing

Most of us get excited about gardening in the spring – the start of the gardening year - when plants are sprouting, the sun shines and we see a few butterflies in the garden. As I became a more experienced gardener, I began to realise that there is no 'start' to the gardening year – gardening is a year round activity and all sorts of

Sweet violet heralds the coming of spring with its scented purple flowers

things begin to happen, at least in a wildlife garden, from December onwards. Seedlings may germinate, the leaves of bulbs start to poke through the soil and a few plants such as violets and hellebores may even come into flower if the weather is mild. The conditions that some wildflower seeds need to break their dormancy occur over the coldest months of the year, so for many species, especially if you are inexperienced, it is a good idea to sow in the autumn from October onwards. If, like me, you sometimes forget to sow in the autumn or winter months, you can often get away with sowing in late February or early March, as long as we are still experiencing frosty weather.

Although there are many wildflower species that need these cold periods, there are also plenty of wildflowers, for instance the campions, which will germinate if they are sown in mild weather in the spring. An appropriate sowing time is given with each of the 'star' species highlighted in Chapters 3 to 9.

What to grow where – looking at your conditions

Bright and vibrant, wild rockrose thrives in a sunny spot

We have already seen that one of the advantages of growing wildflowers is that there will be something beautiful for every situation, from the wettest soil to the driest, and the sunniest spot to the deepest shade. When choosing which plants to grow, first check out your growing conditions. Look at your soil type (sandy, clay, loamy etc), pH (whether your soil is acidic or alkaline – this can be quickly done with a soil testing kit from the garden centre) and how much light or shade there is in different parts of the garden. Then simply choose plants for your local conditions. My previous garden was on a very sandy, free-draining soil, which meant that I was unable to grow plants that required a more moisture retentive substrate. On the positive side, I could grow wild rockrose, musk mallow and common toadflax, which preferred this type of soil. My current garden is quite different with a loamy clay soil, which means that meadowsweet and ragged robin grow well here. Bear in mind though, that many wildflowers are adaptable and further information in this book will indicate which sorts of conditions certain species prefer.

Conserving water

A word here about conserving water in these times of predicted climate change. Many wildflowers are adapted to growing in very dry conditions and some of these can easily be incorporated into our gardens. They require very little in the way of maintenance and will happily exist without watering. Many of the plants suggested for hot sunny borders fall into this category. If you are concerned about conserving water, by growing wildflowers you will be making a positive contribution to that aim.

Getting started

You are now armed with some of the information you need to get started in your wildflower garden. If you decide that you are uncertain about growing from seed, find a good supplier of pot grown wildflowers or plug plants (see page 91), and choose those that are suited to your conditions. The last point you need to consider is that many wildflowers are happiest in relatively poor soils. If you have a garden where compost has been used liberally over the years, you may find that your native species grow rather taller or are more leafy than you would expect. Don't let that put you off. Generally this is only a major problem where a wildflower meadow is to be established and individual plants in borders usually cope well with this extra fertility often producing larger, lusher flowers than their wild cousins. Over time the soil fertility will drop and your plants will happily settle into the conditions.

Designing a wildflower border

Designing a new border of any type is exciting. If you feel particularly inspired, use paper

This wild border contains a mixture of oxeye daisies, foxgloves and hedge cranesbill

and pencil to make rough outlines of the species you wish to plant to produce a planting plan. Get your inspiration from nature, choose groups or combinations of plants that you see together in the countryside and arrange that these are near each other. However, don't plan too meticulously, as it is inevitable that your plants will increase and self seed,

Ragged robin is a wonderful addition to a wildflower border on clay soil

usually producing attractive combinations of shapes and colours that you may not have thought of yourself. Bear in mind that this is likely to happen and allow space between your plants for nature to take its course. You may wish to plant taller wildflowers towards the back of the border, but it is inevitable that the odd tall plant will eventually find its way to the front. This can add interest to a border where varying heights relieve the boredom of plants standing strictly in order of height.

Wildflowers can be incorporated into any garden, filling spaces in more traditional herbaceous borders where they will happily mingle with delphiniums and lupins. They can also be grown in long grass or under hedges in shady spots, or they may be given pride of place in containers and pots. Or you may prefer to establish a special wildflower border, full of the most beautiful of our native species. Whatever you decide, an exciting garden, full of colour and wildlife, lies ahead. Throughout the rest of this book, six star plants are recommended in each of the remaining chapters – plants for sunny borders, shady places, wet areas and grass, climbers for fences or pergolas, plants for containers and some more suitable for a wild spot. These are highlighted in the text as well as having a small section to themselves and a photograph. At the end of each chapter you will find a list of further species that will thrive in that situation. Some plants are mentioned in more than one chapter. This indicates just how versatile many of our wildflowers are.

CHAPTER 3
WILDFLOWERS FOR SUNNY BORDERS

Many of our prettiest wildflowers can be incorporated into sunny places in our gardens, and borders in full sun around even small gardens can be ideal for them. Sunny borders can be made against south facing fences or walls, or in very open situations where they will receive sunlight throughout the day. A dry area in front of a wall can be a particularly difficult situation for more traditional garden plants but there are plenty of drought tolerant sun-loving wildflowers that thrive in these warm, light conditions.

Sowing a cornfield mix

Several of our prettiest wild annuals are suitable for hot sunny spots, including poppy, corn marigold, corn chamomile, corncockle and pheasant's eye. These plants were once common in arable fields, and still appear occasionally where the soil has been recently ploughed or disturbed. As annuals they are best sown directly into the soil where you would like them to establish (they will self sow once they are happy) and together make a fabulous, colourful impact from early summer onwards. After flowering, the variety of tawny-coloured seedheads is impressive, prolonging the interest well into September or even October. These species are well suited to sowing as a mixture, and many suppliers (see page 91) produce a 'cornfield mix' for this purpose. This can be sown in either autumn or early spring. It is important to make sure that the soil is well prepared by removing perennial weeds and raking to a fine tilth. The seed mixture should be scattered as evenly as possible onto the soil surface (if you are sowing a larger area, 2 grams per square meter is an adequate sowing rate), and then gently firmed in. Do not cover the seeds – some of these species require light to trigger germination. Water gently if the weather is dry, but otherwise leave alone. In the autumn the dead seedheads can be pulled out and shaken to distribute the seeds back into the soil and the cycle happily begins again.

Although annuals can bring the almost instant impact of a bright splash of colour to the garden, most of us prefer to grow a variety of perennials in our borders. These longer-lived plants reduce maintenance, can be guaranteed to bloom year after year and require little attention. Perennial wildflowers are no exception and there are many species that are perfect for adding to borders. Indeed there are some that are often grown in gardens and most of us are quite unaware that they are native wildflowers. **Jacob's ladder** is just one example of a British native that has become a garden favourite because of its attractive foliage and bright blue flowers.

Creating and planting a sunny wildflower border

If you intend to plant up a perennial wildflower border from scratch, there are a few initial factors to take into account. Many wildflowers perform really well when the soil is relatively poor, so an area in the garden where turf can be removed is an ideal spot for a new wildflower border, as long as the soil is not too fertile. If you do have very fertile soil, it may be worth removing a few inches of the topsoil and replacing it with poor quality soil from another part of the garden. If you are removing turf, the soil beneath can simply be turned over, and no compost or fertiliser should be added. Annual weed seeds are sure to germinate once the soil is exposed so plan ahead by preparing your area and remove weed seedlings by hoeing or digging out prior to planting your perennial wildflowers. If you are gardening in harmony with your local conditions and are choosing plants that prefer your soil type, no other improvements will need to be made. If you have a very heavy clay soil and would prefer to make it a little more manageable, you could dig in some sharp grit at this stage. If you can, choose a sheltered spot for your border (rather than simply a sunny one), as butterflies in particular prefer to seek their nectar out of the wind.

Whether you intend to purchase plants or grow your own from seed, early spring or late autumn are the best times to start planting your perennial wildflowers. For the back of a sunny border try any of the Verbascums or mulleins, with their huge woolly leaves and yellow flowers. These flowers, which are slightly scented at night, are especially attractive to moths, and one moth species (the aptly named mullein moth) lays her eggs on the grey-green felted leaves. Teasels can also be included in a sunny border, although some people prefer to keep these prolific seeders to a wilder spot (see page 77). **Viper's bugloss**, which buzzes with bees of all kinds in mid summer, is also suitable for the back or mid border. The bright blue of **chicory** complements the pale pink of **musk mallow** – these two plants make a stunning combination and

Viper's bugloss needs a sunny spot and free-draining soil

both cope well with a dry sunny location as will **dark mullein**.

For the mid-border, plants of less stature are required. **Dropwort**, the dry soil equivalent of meadowsweet, is a must and will grow in just about any soil, except wet. Attractive seedheads

follow its frothy white, but sadly unscented, flowers. Other white wildflowers for the mid-border could include wild carrot, with its interesting basket-shaped seed heads, and white campion, a long flowering species. Jacob's ladder will also be happy here, as will wild mignonette (an annual or biennial). Towards the front of the border more dainty flowers can find a home. Heartsease, or wild pansy, with yellow and purple flowers will seed profusely, and lady's bedstraw, wild

Wild carrot has a single magenta flower to attract insects to its pollen

rockrose and bird's foot trefoil all add a splash of yellow from late May onwards.

If you do not wish to start a new area or to plant a border specifically with wildflowers, all the plants above are suitable for adding to existing borders where there are spaces. Choose flower colours that suit the area, add attractive foliage plants such as wild carrot, dropwort or Jacob's ladder or simply include your favourites. They will generally self seed and add something special to an existing perennial border. The cornfield annuals mentioned earlier can also be included in a border. Simply scatter in a little seed after your perennials have been planted. They too will seed over time and establish themselves without any further help from you.

A wildflower border with grasses

The naturalistic style of gardening, where perennials are planted with ornamental grasses, has become extremely popular over the last few years. Its informal look, emphasis on flowing drifts of species and varieties, and ability to cater for wildlife make it an important innovation into more traditional gardening styles. Wildflowers are particularly suitable for inclusion in this type of gardening. But isn't an area of wildflowers and grasses simply

23

a meadow? Not in this instance. This 'new perennial' style involves planting drifts of flowers interspersed with large areas of tufted grasses. A meadow has fine leaved grasses distributed evenly throughout an area and wildflowers scattered here and there. Native

These borders in a wildlife garden contain a mixture of native and cottage garden flowers

grasses could certainly be used in a new perennial style border, but here more dramatic non-natives such as Pennisetum, Stipa and Miscanthus are normally used. If wildflowers and wild grasses are more to your taste Chapter 6 has more information on planting wildflowers into grass.

What not to plant in sunny borders

Not all wildflowers are suitable for planting in our gardens and some should be positively avoided unless you are a real enthusiast. Species that are particularly invasive, either spreading quickly underground or seeding very freely should generally not be included. Some may be suitable for a wilder patch in the garden (see Chapter 9) but others are best left to roadsides and hedgerows unless you are prepared for a lot of work. Several of these invasive wildflowers grow in my garden (in fact they were here when I arrived) but their wildlife attracting capabilities mean that I am happy to accommodate them. However, in a smaller garden they would be very difficult to manage. They include creeping buttercup, hogweed, cow parsley and white deadnettle, all fantastic plants that provide nectar or pollen for insects, but best left out of a sunny border. It is also best to avoid planting rosebay willowherb, common toadflax and coltsfoot – all beautiful but very invasive in this situation.

What wildlife can you expect?

A sunny spot in the garden with plenty of wildflowers will attract a wide range of wildlife. Insects especially will be attracted to such an area as it will be warm and will provide them with the nectar or pollen they will be seeking on sunny days. Butterflies, hoverflies, moths, bumblebees and honeybees will all flock to a sunny wildflower border. Some of the plants, especially chicory, teasel and cornflower will also produce seeds that are favoured by greenfinches and goldfinches. Other birds, including robins, wrens, warblers and thrushes will be drawn to the insects that are making a home in this habitat. Hedgehogs too will seek caterpillars and beetles amongst the plants. Inevitably the wildflowers will bring with them a range of wildlife that shares their natural habitat in the countryside.

Wild marjoram is a magnet for the gatekeeper butterfly

Other plants suitable for sunny areas

Plant name	Latin name	Flowering months	Height	Sowing time	Seed Treatment	
					Cold	Scarify
Basil Thyme	Acinos arvensis	May - Sept	10- 20 cms	Spring		
Clustered Bellflower	Campanula glomerata	June - Aug	15-30 cms	Autumn	✓	✓
Cornflower	Centaurea cyanus	May - Aug	30-100 cms	Spring		
Corn Marigold	Chrysanthemum segetum	June - Sept	20-50 cms	Spring		
Field Poppy	Papaver rhoeas	June - Aug	20-60 cms	Autumn	✓	
Goat's-beard	Tragopogon pratensis	May - July	30-50 cms	Spring		
Great Mullein	Verbascum nigrum	June - Aug	60-200 cms	Autumn		
Perennial Flax	Linum perenne	May - July	30-75 cms	Spring		
Wild Carrot	Daucus carota	June - Sept	30-60 cms	Spring		
Wild Mignonette	Reseda lutea	May - Aug	30-90 cms	Autumn		

Bird's foot trefoil is a valuable butterfly plant

You could also try:

Bird's foot trefoil, bladder campion, field scabious, globeflower, greater knapweed, heartsease, heather, hemp agrimony, hoary plantain, horseshoe vetch, hound's-tongue, kidney vetch, lady's bedstraw, lesser calamint, common knapweed, maiden pink, meadow cranesbill, meadowsweet, pasque flower, perforate St. John's wort, pheasant's eye, purple loosestrife, sainfoin, sea campion, sheep's bit, small scabious, star of Bethlehem, teasel, thrift, vervain, white campion, wild clary, wild parsnip, wild rockrose and yarrow.

Jacobs Ladder   Polemonium caeruleum
This is an easy perennial plant to grow in a sunny spot. Seed germinates quickly without any pre-treatment. The bright blue flowers attract bees in June and July. Also suitable for light shade. Height 30-80 cms.

Dark Mullein   Verbascum nigrum
This perennial plant has a deep tap root. The flowers are yellow with purple centres and appear in tall spikes right through the summer attracting bees and moths. The tiny seeds need some care, but no pre-treatment, to germinate. Height 60-125 cms.

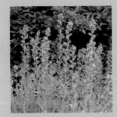

Dropwort   Filipendula vulgaris
A gorgeous frothy white flowered perennial wildflower attracting small insects such as hoverflies in early and mid-summer. The attractive leaves are fern-like in appearance. Seeds germinate easily in spring. Also suitable for a dry meadow. Height 20-50 cms.

Musk Mallow   Malva moschata
Another perennial, musk mallow flowers are a lovely shade of soft pink, complementing many other plants in a border. The flowers appear in mid to late summer, and bring bees and hoverflies to the garden. Seeds germinate sporadically in spring. Also suitable for a dry meadow. Height 30-80 cms.

Viper's Bugloss   Echium vulgare
An excellent bee attractant for a sunny border, its bright blue flowers humming with honeybees, bumblebees and skipper butterflies well into late summer. It is a biennial plant and will self seed well once established. Sow in autumn and move seedlings when small. Height 60-100 cms.

Chicory   Cichorium intybus
Chicory is a biennial which will self sow once established, Its bright blue flowers open on summer mornings but are closed by mid-day. They attract bees, and finches enjoy the seeds. Seeds are easy to germinate in spring with no pre-treatment. Height 30-100 cms.

CHAPTER 4
WILDFLOWERS FOR SHADY PLACES

Every garden has a shady spot somewhere, and this is sometimes the most difficult part of any garden to deal with. Shady places in gardens are often very dry, especially if they are beneath trees, so as gardeners we have to deal with two problems at once. Again our native wildflowers come up trumps, and there are a good number of very attractive plants that will thrive in these situations. If we look to nature for inspiration, we only have to think of a pretty hedge bank full of **stitchwort** and **red campions,** or to remember our last walk in a **bluebell** woodland, to appreciate the array of colourful plants that are suitable for a shady spot. Many of these shade-loving species will flower in springtime or very early in the summer, making them really important for wildlife as well as being plants that will inject a splash of colour into the garden at a time when it is most needed.

The fact that shade tolerant wildflowers can be adaptable is an added bonus and their ability to adjust to varying amounts of light makes this group especially valuable. Red campion for instance will be happy under trees, but may also self-seed out into sunnier spots if it is given the chance. In lighter conditions, red campion may exhibit a paler flower colour than it would in deeper shade, but it is none the less attractive for that and still encourages moths and bees to the garden.

Another great advantage of these shade-lovers is that many of them flower early in the year. If you are looking to maximise the wildlife attracting potential of your garden as a whole, it is important to choose flowering plants that span the seasons. Early insects, straight out of hibernation in March, will be seeking nectar and pollen. Even if attracting wildlife is not a primary aim, a garden with colour throughout the year is something all gardeners strive for. Many of our earliest flowering native species, for example violets and celandines, are plants that are generally found in quite shady habitats. They bloom in spring and produce seeds before the tree canopy has closed up and reduced the amount of light available to them. In a sunny border the majority of wildflowers will be late spring to late summer flowerers, so a shady place in the garden gives us the opportunity grow some early flowers for spring colour and for wildlife.

How much shade?

It is usual when describing the conditions of light and shade in which plants will thrive, to use the terms 'light or semi-shade' or 'deep shade', but what do these terms actually mean and is it necessary to understand them? It is important to appreciate the distinction between light shade and deep shade, as there are plenty of shade tolerant plants that will thrive in light shade, but which will struggle in the deepest shade beneath a beech tree, or in a dark corner behind a shed. We have to give wildflowers the conditions they prefer, even though many are fairly adaptable, and the vast majority of shade lovers prefer light (semi) shade. In this book, light or semi shade refers to shade for up to half the day, or perhaps the dappled shade that exists beneath a birch tree with light foliage. Deep shade means no appreciable direct sunlight at all. This may refer to an area to the north of a house or wall, or the area underneath the canopy of a densely leaved tree in summertime. In springtime of course, before the leaves have unfurled, this sort of area may be quite sunny but shade-loving plants are adapted to these changes in light intensity. Some species, for instance primroses, may even die down and lose their leaves through the mid-summer period when the tree canopy is at its most dense. This is a natural response to the conditions in which they find themselves, and is a means of coping with changes in light levels and moisture availability throughout the year.

Hedges, shrubs and trees in gardens

Bluebell woods can provide inspiration for shady garden corners

Many areas of shade in our gardens are produced by hedges, shrubs and trees, either from our own or our neighbours' plants. If we are 'gardening with nature' we can make use of this environment and turn what may sometimes seem to be adverse conditions to our advantage. An area alongside a neighbour's tall hedge can be turned into a shady walkway, full of colourful flowers in spring and early summer, and lush and green with wood rush, ferns and the leaves of wild hellebores in mid and late summer. Some plants, for example the **stinking hellebore** and pendulous sedge, can create a swathe of green leaves through the winter, and the sedge also has elegant drooping seedheads that add to the almost tropical effect that can be achieved in shady spots. In springtime, primroses, sweet woodruff and yellow archangel will add colour, and **foxgloves** in early summer will feed bumblebees galore as well as inject a splash of pink that lasts for several weeks. An area that could have presented a problem has been turned into a special shady habitat not unlike a hedgerow or the edge of a woodland thanks to our native flora.

Creating a shady wildflower border

An area such as the one described above can be created in any space where light is lacking, whether it be alongside the wall of a house, under trees or beside a tall hedge. Very tall Leyland cypress hedges are a particular problem as the shade they cast is very dense and they reduce the soil alongside them to dust by removing available water and nutrients. This means that only plants that tolerate deep shade and extremely dry conditions will survive alongside these plants, and even amongst our versatile wildflowers there are only a few species that can cope in these conditions. I have had some success with wild strawberry and hedge woundwort, but in view of the problems Leyland cypress cause they are best replaced with a wildlife friendly hedge of native shrubs and climbers. If the hedge happens to be in a neighbour's garden, diplomatic negotiations to reduce the height (now required by law) are the best approach. This at least will allow more light into your garden. When planting beneath a Leyland cypress hedge, choose from the wildflowers that prefer deep shade, and keep the soil around them well mulched with organic matter. These dense hedges are not totally wildlife unfriendly – in fact they attract a wide range of nesting birds, provide sheltering places for over-wintering insects such as ladybirds and, like all conifers can encourage one of our most beautiful native birds, the goldcrest, into our gardens.

Wild strawberry will flower and fruit in deep shade

Areas alongside a house wall may also be extremely dry, so care must be taken with plants in these places. Mulch well in autumn and again in spring if necessary, and water the plants in the summer until they are established. Many shade-loving species cope well with dry conditions once they are settled and even if wilting occurs on hot days, they perk up again as the temperature drops. Mulching helps to lock in the soil moisture and prevent the extremes of dryness that can cause plants to fail completely.

Starting an area like this from scratch is relatively easy. Often there is little vegetation in these dry, dark places anyway, so there is no need to spend effort and time removing grass or existing plants. The soil should be improved with organic compost if it is dust-like. Well-rotted bark is also excellent as it reproduces a woodland floor habitat and encourages some of the wildlife – small mammals, insects and other invertebrates – that inhabit these places in the countryside.

Planting in deep shade

Nature can again influence your choice of plants for these areas and a walk in a beech or oak woodland will give you a good idea of the types of wildflowers that can cope

with these conditions. These two tree species cast heavy shade from late spring until the autumn, so plants for this type of area need to be especially adapted to low light levels. An obvious first choice is the bluebell, a stunning native bulb with a deep blue spike of nodding flowers in May. Bluebells can be planted in September and October and should be obtained from a reputable grower of native bulbs (see suppliers list on page 91). Many bulbs are still being taken from the wild, so make sure your supplier can assure their provenance. Also avoid Spanish bluebells. Although these are quite attractive plants in their own right, they cross pollinate with our own wild species and cause the dilution of the genetic stock of our native plants.

Stinking hellebore provides year round interest of flowers and evergreen foliage

Another stunning wildflower that copes well with deep shade is the stinking hellebore. This is a striking evergreen plant with deeply dissected shiny leaves, and drooping clusters of pale green flowers, each one tipped with a rim of maroon around the petals. Its real advantage lies in its ability to flower at the end of winter, just when we are looking forward to spring. Our other native hellebore, the green hellebore, is an equally attractive but smaller plant. Once established both species will self-seed and spread slowly, and seedlings can be moved to other parts of the garden when they are large enough to handle. These two plants look particularly good when combined with the wild wood rush, or the pendulous sedge, the latter being a plant of many different habitats in the wild. Some of the native cranesbills can also cope with these dark conditions, in particular the dainty herb Robert, with its ferny leaves and small bright pink flowers. Mourning widow, a pretty cranesbill with dark maroon flowers, also handles the shade well. In addition you could try wood anemone or wood sorrel, both early to bloom with pure white, open flowers. For attractive foliage there are many native ferns, such as hart's tongue and male fern also which will do well in deeply shady spots. For thick ground cover where little else will grow, ivy works well, clothing bare dry soil with a swathe of glossy dark green leaves. If a splash of bright yellow in spring appeals you could introduce lesser celandine, although most gardeners avoid it on account of its ability to spread like wildfire!

Planting in light shade

If the shade beside your house, hedge or shrubs or beneath neighbouring trees is light or dappled, there are almost endless possibilities. As we have already seen the majority of our native shade-loving plants flower early in the spring or summer, as this is their strategy for coping with a shady habitat, but it is possible with some careful planning to find plants that will provide colour for many months of the year.

Snowdrops are perhaps the best choice for the earliest of bulbs, but are they native? The jury is still out on that one, and it is possible that they were introduced, so whether you include them in a wildflower garden or not is your choice. Many wildflower gardeners mix natives and non-natives anyway, and it would be a shame to miss out on the thrill of the first snowdrop for the sake of our lack of knowledge of the origins of this wonderful little bulb. Next in the season would be the wild violets, and both dog violet and **sweet violet** are good choices for light shade. Both seed well and will move into less shady areas of their own accord. Primroses too will flower in early spring and they combine well with violets, especially on a shady bank. As spring progresses, a wealth of wildflowers come into their own. You could include greater stitchwort, Welsh poppy, garlic mustard, hedge cranesbill, yellow archangel, wild daffodil, lily of the valley, Solomon's seal and oxlip. Sweet cicely, sweet woodruff, wild strawberry, garlic

Foxgloves enjoy the light shade beneath a silver birch

mustard, nettle leaved bellflower, ramsons and wood spurge also flower between spring and early summer, depending on the area of the country in which you live. The majority of these woodland beauties have white or yellow flowers, so the blossoming of pink red campion and foxglove comes as a contrast in May, especially when combined with the glorious blue of our native bluebell. The wild columbine, which has deep purple flowers, looks especially good with red campion alongside.

*With glorious scent as well as beautiful flowers, meadowsweet
will grow in light shade in heavy soil*

Several other plants provide interest in the mid-summer months. Stinking iris, also known as roast beef plant on account of the strange smell of its leaves, flowers early in the year, but displays its large bright orange seeds through the summer months. The wild strawberry too adds a splash of colour at this time with its tiny red fruits, if the blackbirds don't get them first. Two more wild geraniums, the wood cranesbill and bloody cranesbill add more summer colour, and teasels, which tolerate light shade or full sun begin to open their

Herb Robert combines well with sweet woodruff

pink flowers in July and continue to provide interest right through the winter.

In addition to these light shade specialists, many of the species mentioned as suitable for deep shade will also do well here, so there are a great many beautiful wildflowers to choose from for this particular habitat.

Planting in grass

Where a light covering of grass exists under trees it is possible to add wildflowers to produce a very attractive effect. It could be a question of trial and error, as the success or otherwise of this will depend upon the density and species of grass, as well as the wildflowers you choose. Primrose, sweet violet, red campion, hedge woundwort and teasel will all establish in grassy areas, but many of the other species mentioned are happier growing in an area of leaf mould or composted bark, which is most like the conditions in their natural habitat beneath trees.

What not to plant

As with the sunny areas already discussed, there are wildflowers to avoid in this situation. Lesser celandine is probably one that should be planted with caution (although I love it) as in a small garden it really can take over. Cow parsley, or Queen Anne's lace, is also best avoided, although again it is a beautiful plant. Teasels can seed rather too freely for some tastes, and of course the non-native Spanish bluebell should be excluded.

Lesser celandine brightens the spring garden but spreads rapidly

What wildlife can you expect?

Shady areas have a whole array of interesting creatures associated with them, and many of these are rather different from the bees and butterflies we tend to see in sunnier spots in the garden. There are a few butterfly species that may frequent these shadier places, especially if they are associated with a hedgerow. The speckled wood is a butterfly that spends most of its time in dappled shade, and the orange tip lays her eggs on the wildflower garlic mustard (also called Jack-by-the-hedge), which grows in a lightly shady habitat. Several of the plants mentioned attract bumblebees, especially foxgloves, the wild cranesbills, teasel and yellow archangel. The cranesbills also have large nutritious seeds which finches love – in my former garden a family of bullfinches arrived in May and June every year to take the seeds from herb Robert (which may produce the odd flower at almost any time of year), wood cranesbill and mourning widow. Other birds too frequent slightly shadier places to find food or even to nest. Robins, wrens, blackbirds and thrushes will all search for food under trees or hedges, as will many small mammals, especially hedgehogs. This in part is due to the wealth of insects and other invertebrates that find a home in the cool, damp layer of leaves and bark that builds up in these areas. If you can, add to these layers with home made compost or leaf mould and you will be enhancing the habitat still more for the wildlife that uses it. If your shady place is alongside a wall or behind a garden shed rather than beneath trees, create a habitat by adding leaf mould, composted bark and even a pile of logs to encourage the invertebrates that provide food for woodland birds and mammals.

The wild cranesbills, including this wood cranesbill, make stunning garden plants in sun or shade

Other plants suitable for shady places

Plant name	Latin name	Flowering months	Height	Sowing time	Seed Treatment	
					Cold	Scarify
Green Hellebore	Helleborus viridis	Feb - Mar	40–50 cms	Autumn	✓	
Hedge Cranesbill	Geranium pyreniacum	June - Sept	30-90 cms	Spring		✓
Herb Robert	Geranium robertianum	Feb - Oct	10-40 cms	Spring		✓
Pendulous Sedge	Carex pedula	May - Aug	50-120 cms	Spring		
Primrose	Primula vulgaris	Mar - May	10-20 cms	Autumn	✓	
Sweet Cicely	Myrrhis odorata	May - June	40-90 cms	Autumn	✓	
Welsh Poppy	Meconopsis cambrica	May - July	30-60 cms	Autumn		
Wild Columbine	Aquilegia vulgaris	May - July	30-90 cms	Autumn	✓	
Wild Strawberry	Fragaria vesca	Apr - June	5-25 cms	Spring		
Wood Rush	Luzula sylvatica	Apr - June	20-80 cms	Autumn		

You could also try:

Betony, bloody cranesbill, bugle, common comfrey, dog violet, garlic mustard, hedge bedstraw, hedge woundwort, hart's tongue fern, ivy, lesser celandine, lily of the valley, lords and ladies, lungwort, meadow cranesbill, meadowsweet, mourning widow, nettle-leaved bellflower, oxlip, perforate St. John's wort, ramsons, royal fern, selfheal, solomon's seal, stinking iris, sweet woodruff, teasel, tufted vetch, water avens, wild cyclamen, wild daffodil, wood anemone, wood avens, wood cranesbill, wood sage, wood sorrel, wood spurge, wood vetch, yellow archangel.

Welsh poppy will seed and spread well in light shade

Greater Stitchwort   Stellaria holostea

A beautiful creeping perennial species with starry white flowers in late spring and early summer. Bees are attracted to this plant, which will also grow in sun in fertile soil. The seeds germinate easily in spring with no pre-treatment. Height 10-50 cms.

Bluebell   Endymion non-scriptus

Bluebells are easy to grow from bulbs in deep or light shade or even in full sun, although their colour is paler in sunny spots. The flowers are visited by bees and some butterflies in May. Seed should be sown in autumn, as frosty conditions are needed to break dormancy. Height 25-30 cms.

Red Campion   Silene dioica

One of the easiest wildflowers to establish in light shade. The pink flowers appear from late April until July and sporadically thereafter, and attract bees and especially moths. Seeds germinate easily in spring with no pre-treatment. Also suitable for sunny spots. Height 30-100 cms.

Stinking Hellebore   Helleborus foetidus

An evergreen perennial, the stinking hellebore is great value in light or deep shade with glossy green leaves all year and green flowers in late winter and spring. Excellent for early pollen for insects. Sow seeds in autumn, as they need frosty conditions to germinate. Height 30-90 cms.

Sweet Violet   Viola odorata

A breath of spring when we most need it, the purple scented flowers of this perennial plant appear as early as February and continue into April. Plants produce runners and can be easily split or divided, or the seeds may be sown in the autumn. Also suitable for containers Height 8-15 cms.

Foxglove   Digitalis purpurea

One of our most beautiful wildflowers with huge spikes of pink flowers, providing pollen for bumblebees in May and June. This biennial plant produces masses of tiny seeds, which will increase your plants of their own accord. Alternatively sow in spring. Height 60-160 cms.

CHAPTER 5
WILDFLOWERS FOR WET PLACES

Damp or wet places in our gardens can be particularly difficult conditions in which to grow an attractive selection of plants, but there are plenty of wildflowers that are suitable for these soil conditions. Some gardeners despair of these wet patches - even to the point of installing drainage to correct the 'problem'. But for the wildflower gardener these drastic measures are unnecessary, as a damp lawn can be filled with cowslips and **snakeshead fritillaries** to create a stunning spring meadow effect, or a wet hollow may be converted into a bog garden, full of water mint, **purple loosestrife** and **ragged robin**. Wet places in gardens should be regarded as chances not to be missed rather than problems to be solved.

It is worth remembering that other aspects of these wet spots need to be taken into account, especially the consideration of light and shade. As we have already seen, within any habitat there will always be wildflowers that prefer full sun and others that have a preference for less light. Plants must be chosen with care in order that they give of their best in any situation.

What do we mean by 'wet places'?

First and foremost what do we actually mean by a 'wet' habitat? In this chapter we can consider a range of situations from deep water in a wildflower pond, through shallow water or permanently boggy soil, to the classic clay soil - very wet in the winter, but drying out in summer. These wetter places may occur naturally in your garden, or you may wish to create damper habitats for the purpose of attracting wildlife. Either way, wetter spots will enable you to grow some of our most attractive wildflower species.

Wildflowers in ponds

A pond in the garden, whether it is a special wildlife habitat or a more formal pool, is an ideal situation to try some wetland wildflowers. We are fortunate in having a wealth of stunning species for these damper spots and many of them have bright colourful flowers in shades of yellow, pink and purple. If you have a formal pond, the water depth is likely to be fairly uniform. This means that only plants that survive in water of perhaps 30 cm or more will be suitable for a pond of this type. The numbers of native plants that will thrive in a steep sided pond are rather restricted, but there are still some that are suitable. For the deepest water the native white water lily is a good choice, but only if the pond is large. This is a plant that needs plenty of space and can be invasive, but this aside, its pure white flowers with their bright yellow central boss of stamens, surrounded by deep green glossy leaves, provide a stunning sight that enhances any large pond, whether formal or natural. Other wildflowers suitable for a formal pond include several species that can be planted into large containers. Bogbean, with small, fringed white flowers or the beautiful pink-blossomed flowering rush are both suitable as are the larger sedges including cyperus sedge, pendulous sedge, or the luxuriant sweet galingale. These species should be planted in containers and positioned on bricks or stones to raise them up to a suitable height, to ensure that the soil level in the container is about 10cms below the water surface.

No pond is complete without a water lily, but our native white lily needs lots of space

A wildlife pond rather than a formal pool opens up many more possibilities. A habitat of this sort is generally constructed with gently sloping edges, creating varying water depths, plus areas of wet soil on the margins. A wide range of wildflowers can be planted into these different areas, including those that prefer the wet soil on the pond edge such as the pink flowered ragged robin and purple loosestrife or the bright yellow marsh marigold. Delicate fringed water lily with its lily pad leaves and frilly yellow flowers or the white flowered frogbit, are happy in the open water. The list of wetland plants at the end of this chapter will give you some ideas of other species that you could include in a wildlife pond.

If you do not have a pond in your garden but wish to create one, there are recommended books on page 90 with information to help you decide what sort of pond is right for you, and how to construct it.

Wildflowers in bog gardens

If a pond is not suitable for your particular circumstances, you may prefer the idea of a bog garden, where some wetland species will thrive, but there is no actual open water. This can be an option in gardens where small children play, or if you would prefer not to have the maintenance associated with a pond. A bog garden will provide the perfect place for a great variety of native plants and if you are interested in the wildlife that may come to your garden, a boggy area will still supply a damp, shady place for frogs, toads and newts to spend the summer, and a variety of invertebrates will inhabit these wet spots, both deep in the soil and on its surface. These latter creatures provide food for many birds and mammals, including hedgehogs as well as amphibians.

The majority of wildflowers that are suitable for wet soil at the pond edge, including hemp agrimony, angelica, valerian and comfrey, all look wonderful in a bog garden. The varying flower hues and leaf shapes of these species make a colourful combination with interest for many months of the year. A bog garden 'island bed' can easily be created in damp grass. In this case you may wish to plant the taller species mentioned above in the middle, and shorter species such as the delicate mauve **lady's smock** and spring flowering **bugle** with its spikes of purple flowers, on the edges, grading the heights to give a good view of all the plants from every angle. However, many of these plants will spread and

This damp spot in a wildlife garden supports purple loosestrife and common fleabane

seed, and soon your bog garden will take on a structure of its own, so it may not be worth planning too meticulously. It will look all the more attractive for being allowed to develop over time.

If you have a naturally damp spot that would be suitable for a wildflower bog garden, you have an advantage over gardeners with dry soil. Turf can be removed from such an area to define your border and your chosen species planted. In drier soils it is necessary to create an area where water will be retained by using a rubber or polythene pond liner. A boggy place such as this is relatively easy to create by removing existing soil to a depth of between 30 and 60 cms, easing a flexible liner into the hole, and replacing the soil. However, even a bog garden needs to have some through flow of water to prevent the soil becoming stagnant and unhealthy, so drainage holes need to be made in the liner before the soil goes back in. This can be done with a garden fork, by methodically pushing the tines through the liner all over the bottom of the area. To give the plants a boost and create a really attractive area with a wealth of luxuriant plants, a layer of garden compost can be added if you wish at this stage, before refilling with garden soil. For more information on the creation of a bog garden, turn to page 90 for useful books. If your soil is naturally wet, simply remove weeds from the area (or turf if it is grassed) and plant your selection of wetland wildflowers. A thin mulch of organic compost will get everything off to a great start, and help to retain the natural moisture.

Wet or clay soils

Clay soils have a habit of drying out severely if the summer months are dry, but in general the plants mentioned in this chapter, with the obvious exceptions of those requiring deep water, have the ability to cope with this. In the wild many wetland plants that grow naturally in clay soils are well adapted to this wet in winter/dry in summer regime. You may wish to combine wetland wildflowers with colourful non-natives that also prefer a damper soil – irises, bergamot, Primula, Rodgersia or Astilbe - to make a really attractive combination

of shapes and colours. If this blend of native and non-native appeals to you, choose non-invasive wildflowers such as dark purple devil's-bit scabious, delicate nodding water avens and bugle, which complement each other and are relatively easy to keep under control. Water mint will also grow in damp soil of this type, but can spread quite quickly; however with its wonderful fragrance, puffs of pink flowers, and ability to attract butterflies and bees, you can't really have too much of it.

Cowslips and bugle flower at the same time, creating a stunning contrast

Wildflowers in wet grass

Wildflowers can also be planted into a wet lawn. This can turn a difficult problem into an attractive feature. The most appropriate species for a wet spring 'meadow' include the snakeshead fritillary, cowslip, lady's smock and bugle – all easy to establish and able to cope in most lawn grasses. If you have an older lawn with fine leaved species of grass such as the fescues, you could also add ragged robin,

Lady's smock will spread rapidly in a damp meadow

frothy white **meadowsweet** with its heavenly scent or water avens. There are many species that will thrive in this sort of situation, but do make sure you have information about looking after the area. It will need to be cut and raked at least once every year or the wildflowers will slowly disappear. Books that have information on maintaining meadow areas are listed on page 90.

Wildflowers for stream sides

A few lucky gardeners might have a small natural stream running through their garden. This is a great place to establish some wildflowers, but the situation is rather different from the habitats described above. Flowing water brings its own problems, and plants that grow in the wild in these sorts of places are adapted to changes in water levels, as well as having the ability to cope with the water movement without being washed away. On damp banks, any of the plants mentioned for bog gardens or wet or clay soil will cope, but plants for flowing water need to be chosen carefully. As far as our native species are concerned, greater spearwort with its large yellow buttercup flowers, yellow flag (also called wild iris) water mint, marsh marigold and many of the native rushes and sedges, are all suitable. For the fast flowing water in the middle of a shallow stream, the various species of water crowsfoot and the yellow water lily, or brandy bottle would do well.

Wildflowers for mini-ponds and mini-bogs

Wetland wildflowers can be grown in even the smallest garden if you choose species that are slow growing and therefore suitable for containers. A mini-pond in an

attractive ceramic container or a wooden half barrel is a lovely small habitat for a patio and will attract birds to drink and bathe as well as the occasional dragonfly or damselfly. It is important here to grow only the smallest wildflowers to avoid your pond being taken over. I particularly like lesser spearwort, water crowsfoot and brooklime, which are suitable for planting into pots or baskets to stand in the container. Lesser spearwort has pretty yellow buttercup-type flowers but is not as invasive as its greater spearwort cousin. Brooklime has bright blue flowers which blend well with the tiny white stars of the crowsfoot. Plant these species into individual pots and cover the compost with a layer of gravel.

This barrel mini-pond has various wetland plants including the white flowered water crowsfoot

To prepare your container, place a layer of gravel or flat pieces of brick or stone in the bottom in order to raise the potted plants to a suitable water depth – the surface of the pots should be a few centimeters beneath the water surface. The depth is not crucial and the water level will fluctuate with evaporation anyway – these plants are very adaptable and will cope with varying conditions as long as they do not dry out completely. As well as potted plants try to include some with surface leaves. The delicate free-floating frogbit with its small white flowers is a perfect container plant if you can find a supplier. If you would like some round water lily shaped leaves, the tiny yellow flowered fringed water lily is ideal. I also use duckweed in a mini-pond of this type. It shades the water, helping to keep it cool, clear and algae-free, but is easily scooped off if it spreads too quickly. A handful of a native oxygenator such as hornwort will also help to keep the water clean and fresh.

A mini bog can be made in a similar way. Check that there are drainage holes in this container and stand it in a large plant pot saucer. Top up the saucer with rainwater from time to time to ensure that the mini-bog stays damp, but not completely waterlogged. Good peat-free compost with added humus should be used to ensure that water is retained. Try delicate ragged robin, cowslip, devil's-bit scabious and bugle for a lovely combination of colours. Any wildflowers for bogs or wet soil will be happy in a container of this sort, but make sure nothing too large or invasive is added.

What not to plant

As with all the other garden areas mentioned, there are plenty of wildflowers that are best avoided in wet situations. Many wildflowers that are supplied with everything they need to grow will spread rapidly, and this is particularly true of wetland plants. With unlimited water at their disposal, some species grow very quickly. Avoid water parsnip, yellow flag and greater spearwort unless you have a natural stream in your garden. Bulrushes of any sort, sweet galingale except in a tough container, branched bur-reed and butterbur are also very invasive. Bogbean can also spread vigorously, but is relatively easy to pull out if it starts to take over.

The feathery petalled flowers of bogbean in close-up

Propagating water plants

Although many of the bog and wet soil plants are easy to grow from seed, most wildflowers for ponds are easier to divide and re-plant when they are in full growth. Often small pieces of wetland wildflowers, such as fringed water lily, bogbean and frogbit can be obtained from friends, but make sure that you are happy with their identity before adding to your own wetland area. Many an invasive thug has been introduced inadvertently in this way!

What wildlife can you expect?

Wet places are especially important to our native wildlife. Birds, mammals, frogs, toads, newts, and insects of all types (especially dragonflies and damselflies) will visit open water to drink, bathe or breed. The occasional grass snake may put in an appearance. The amphibians and reptiles will also find damp places such as bog gardens and wet lawns attractive. In addition some of the wildflowers suitable for these areas are excellent bee and butterfly attractants. Water mint, hemp agrimony, fleabane, lady's smock, bugle, ragged robin, purple loosestrife and gipsywort all provide nectar or pollen for insects. Lady's smock is also the caterpillar food plant for the beautiful orange tip butterfly. You can find out more about the wildlife that might be drawn to a garden wetland in any of the wildlife gardening books on page 90. Including water in the garden is one of the most effective ways we can help our local wildlife. Growing wetland wildflowers in these damp places makes wet habitats even more valuable, as well as providing them with a really natural beauty.

Other plants suitable for wet places

Plant name	Latin name	Flowering months	Height	Sowing time	Seed Treatment Cold	Scarify
Brooklime	Veronica beccabunga	May – Aug	20-30 cms	Spring		
Common Fleabane	Pulicaria dysenterica	July – Sept	30-60 cms	Spring		
Cyperus Sedge	Carex pseudocyperus	May – June	60-100 cms	Spring		
Devil's-bit Scabious	Succisa pratensis	July – Sept	30-60 cms	Spring		
Flowering Rush	Butomus umbellatus	July – Sept	100-150 cms	Autumn	✓	
Fringed Water Lily	Nymphoides peltata	May – Sept	3-6 cms	Spring		
Frogbit	Hydrocaris morsus-ranae	July – Aug	3-6 cms			
Lesser Spearwort	Ranunculus flammula	May – July	30-60 cms	Autumn		
Marsh Marigold	Caltha palustris	Mar – May	25-45 cms	Autumn	✓	
Water Mint	Mentha aquatica	July - Oct	15-60 cms	Spring	✓	

You could also try:

Amphibious bistort, angelica, arrowhead, bogbean, common comfrey, common valerian, cowslip, duckweed, gipsywort, grass of Parnassus, globeflower, greater bird's foot trefoil, greater spearwort, hemp agrimony, marshmallow, pendulous sedge, royal fern, sweet galingale, water avens, water crowsfoot, water forget-me-not, water plantain, water violet, white water lily, yellow flag, yellow loosestrife, yellow water lily (brandy bottle).

Water crowsfoot has white flowers which stand above the water surface

Ragged Robin
Lychnis flos-cuculi
A pretty, delicate wildflower with masses of ragged dark pink flowers in early summer. It attracts bees and moths to its nectar. The seeds germinate easily in the spring with no pre-treatment. Also suitable for a damp meadow. Height 30-50 cms.

Lady's Smock
Cardamine pratensis
Lady's smock or cuckoo flower has pale mauve-pink flowers in late spring. This is an important wildlife plant, being the caterpillar food plant of the orange tip butterfly. Bees and butterflies also visit the flowers. The seed germinates well in spring. Also suitable for a damp meadow. Height 20-50 cms.

Bugle
Ajuga reptans
Bugle is a creeping perennial plant with glossy green leaves and spikes of small bright purple flowers in springtime. It makes excellent ground cover in a damp shady place, attracting bees and butterflies. Seed should be sown in autumn, but this wildflower is easy to grow from runners. Also suitable for a shady spot. Height 10-20 cms.

Meadowsweet
Filipendula ulmaria
A perennial wildflower with a fabulous perfume, the meadowsweet has creamy white flowers which fill the garden with scent from early to late summer . A few bees and butterflies will visit the flowers and birds eat the seeds. Germinates well in spring. Also suitable for a wet meadow. Height 60-100 cms.

Purple Loosestrife
Lythrum salicaria
One of our most beautiful wildflowers, purple loosestrife prefers a sunny wet spot, where its tall spikes of dark pink flowers look spectacular combined with meadowsweet. It flowers throughout the summer. The tiny seeds should be sown in spring on the surface of the compost, and not covered at all. They germinate easily if kept moist. Height 50-120 cms.

Snakeshead Fritillary
Fritillaria meleagris
This familiar flower has a pure white form as well as the purple chequered bells we are more familiar with. Bumblebees visit for nectar and pollen in spring. Seeds should be sown in autumn and germinate easily the following spring, but may take up to 5 years to reach flowering size so bulbs are a better option. Also suitable for a damp meadow. Height 20-35 cms.

CHAPTER 6
WILDFLOWERS FOR GRASSY PLACES

Most of us have some grassy places in our gardens whether it be a tiny lawn or a verdant expanse of rye grass. Many gardeners love the flat uninterrupted green of a lawn whilst to others, the idea that rather boring stretches of green grass can become more meadow-like, is very appealing. This chapter however is not about creating a wildflower meadow - it is more about making the grass in our gardens a little more colourful in spring and summer. A proper wild meadow is a very special habitat consisting of an amazing community of plants - as many as 100 native species in one square metre. This diversity of species builds up over many years, and the meadow's structure and the plant species in it, are dependent upon many things including the intervention of both man and beast. The type of soil beneath the plants is also very important. If something approximating a wild meadow is your ultimate aim, some of the books on page 90 will have information on how to create one from a mixture of grass and wildflower seed.

However, if we have grassy areas in our gardens we may wish to encourage a community of plants that slowly becomes a little like a meadow. This chapter is about planting perennial wildflower plants that are suitable for our soil type, into grassy places such as lawns and banks. It is worth mentioning here that wildflower seeds, scattered onto grass, will not grow! You will simply be wasting your seeds (and our money) if you attempt to establish wildflowers in this way. Also, only perennial wildflowers grow really well in grass. Annual wildflowers such as poppies and cornflowers will not establish in an area such as this. They are best grown in a sunny border and there is more information about them in Chapter 3.

Types of grass

Firstly though it is important to know what sort of grass you have. Many lawn grass mixtures are composed of tough hard-wearing species, in particular rye grass, which make establishing wildflowers rather difficult. If this is the sort of lawn you have in your garden your choice of wildflowers is severely restricted. However it is still possible to find some plants that will survive in competition with these fast growing, tough grasses. If your grass area is wet, turn to Chapter 5 which deals especially with wetter soils. There you will find recommendations of plants that suit this type of habitat. For grassy areas in light or deep shade, there are suggestions of suitable plants in Chapter 4. If you have an area in your garden that is wild and a bit overgrown, perhaps with tall, tussocky or rough leaved grasses, do not despair. There are still strong wildflowers that can cope with the competition that these wilder areas create. This type of habitat, which is especially good for wildlife, is covered in Chapter 9.

Adding wildflowers to rye grass areas

But firstly how do we deal with rye grass lawns? Our problem here is that this particular grass is strong and competitive and leaves little room for wildflowers to find a niche to survive. Wildflower seeds from surrounding areas may fall upon it in the summer, but will be unable to get down to the soil to germinate. Many delicate wildflowers planted into rye grass will eventually die out and disappear, (if they establish at all) so we need to choose our species carefully for this habitat. One ally for the wildflower gardener is the **cowslip**, a tough, versatile and beautiful flower. Its ability to survive in dry, wet and grassy conditions make it a perfect choice to add colour and fragrance to a rye grass lawn. It is able to survive the vigorous nature of the grass because it dies down in late spring after it has flowered, losing its leaves and spending much of the summer in a dormant state just on the soil surface to reappear in September. The grass can be cut during the summer without damaging the cowslip plants. Primroses will also survive reasonably well in rye grass, but the best companion for the cowslip in this situation would be a selection of wild bulbs. We have only a few native bulbs that are easy to obtain, but the wild daffodil is perfect for this situation and several growers supply nursery-cultivated bulbs (not taken from the wild). If the grass is damp or on a clay substrate, you could also try snakeshead fritillary. The juxtaposition of purple-chequered drooping fritillary flowers with the pale

Cowslips are easy wildflowers to grow in grass of any type

yellow cowslip bells is a classic combination once found in many riverside meadows in Central England. A wildflower and rye grass area such as this can be cut in June when the seeds have dropped and bulbs and cowslips are safe from harm.

Sunny lawns without rye grass

Most of us have a vision in our minds of a true meadow – a grassy area, full of wildflowers and dancing with butterflies in the summer sunshine. While we can't reproduce this vision in our gardens, we can at least enhance lawns, especially if they are composed of fine leaved grasses. A lawn like this may already have small wildflowers in it, but if it is constantly mown we may never see them flower. Allowing an area such as this to grow up uncut from April until the summer should give an idea of which species are already thriving there. You could see daisies, buttercups, selfheal and plantains, and possibly several other species if you live in an older house. Sometimes old lawns contain lady's bedstraw, medick, various vetches and trefoils, even orchids in some instances, and if allowed to grow and flower these areas can make pretty wildflower lawns without a great deal of establishment work on your part. A simple path mown through them enhances the effect. An area such as this can benefit enormously from the further addition of small wildflower plants, either those you have grown

In close-up the hoary plantain has attractive pink flowers

yourself or plug plants from a supplier. Plantains may not inspire your imagination, but the **hoary plantain** is a wonderful plant with spikes of fluffy pale pink flowers that persist for weeks in the summer. It takes its name from the rosettes of flat, grey green leaves that are covered in soft hairs. These leaves spread over time to make little mats, each with several pink fluffy flower spikes.

There are many other plants suitable for sunny grass that does not contain rye if you are happy with a taller meadow effect. **Oxeye daisy** (or moon daisy) is perfect for a tall flowery lawn of this sort and is very easy to grow from seed. **Field scabious** and **greater knapweed** are two very hardy species that can cope with most soil types. Their mauve and purple flowers (respectively) brighten a grassy area from mid summer through to late September and attract a great range of wildlife, especially butterflies. Knapweed also has seeds that are relished by goldfinches, so birds as well as insects will visit a garden lawn such as this. Other good species for inclusion in a grassy area are lady's bedstraw, mouse-ear hawkweed, bird's foot trefoil, St. John's wort and meadow vetching, all with yellow flowers. For white flowers you could try yarrow (many lawns already have this) wild carrot and bladder campion.

Grassy banks

Some gardeners are fortunate enough to have in their garden a grassy bank that slopes towards the sun. This is a great asset as it lends itself perfectly to the addition of smaller wildflowers. Primroses are the obvious choice, and both sweet and dog violets too will produce a lovely spring spectacle. If you can obtain plants or grow your own from seed, the bird's-eye primrose will add a touch of pink in early summer. Bird's foot trefoil would also do well here, as would lady's bedstraw, but sadly none of these species will cope well with rye grass.

How to add plug plants

If you have already got the hang of growing your own wildflowers from seed and have pricked the seedlings out into plugs, you are in a perfect position to create your own flowery lawn. Plugs can also be purchased from several specialist growers and the details of some of these are on page 91. The best time to add these small plants to a grassy area is autumn, although early spring can also be fine, but they will need watering through the drier weather. The important point is that the job is done when the grass is short, either just after it has been cut at the end of the summer (see the next section on maintenance) or before things really start to grow in the springtime. The most useful implement for this

Later in summer this verdant meadow will be bursting with wildflowers

*The pinks and mauves of field scabious and wild marjoram fill a summer
meadow with colour and wildlife*

task is a bulb planter, which can be used to create a small hole. A small plug of soil is then lifted out and the little plant is tucked into the space. Push a little extra soil down the sides of the hole, settle the plant in and water well. You may need to continue to water if the weather is dry, so this is another good reason to do your planting when the grass is short. Once the grass has grown, it will be difficult to water the small plants without trampling your new flowery area.

One man went to mow

It is important to consider the maintenance of any grass in the garden before you begin to convert all your lawns to wildflower sanctuaries. There is maintenance involved in order to keep your wildflowers flourishing and this can be hard work! It really isn't just a question of planting your chosen species and letting them get on with it. The area must be cut at least once every year, in order to keep the grasses under control and ensure that the wildflowers have a chance to flourish. The best time to do this is in late summer when the majority of the wildflowers will have finished flowering and dropped their seeds. The best implement to carry out this vital work is probably an old fashioned scythe – not something many of us have tucked away in the garden shed! A hand sickle can be used for smaller areas, or an Allen scythe or motorised scythe can be hired from a tool hire company. The key to the success of this operation is cutting the grass as cleanly as possible - this enables the hay to be easily raked off later. After cutting, the grass can lie for a few days to dry, allowing seeds to drop and giving any invertebrates in the hay a chance to find their way to safety. Raking the hay off must be done vigorously, taking away as much of the cut grass and other plants as possible. Exposing small areas of bare soil by raking firmly will provide spaces for seeds to find the soil surface and germinate, in order to continually renew both grasses and wildflowers. An area such as this is a very

dynamic habitat and its composition changes from one season to the next. If this maintenance work is not regularly carried out, over time the wildflowers will slowly disappear and your lawn may return to grass alone. Several of the books listed on page 90 will give you more detailed information on how to maintain your flowery lawn to ensure that it continues to develop over time.

It has already been mentioned that rich soil can cause wildflowers to grow rather larger than they normally would in their natural habitats, although in some situations this is not a problem. In your lawn however it is possible that the grasses, especially if you have used fertiliser it over the years, may grow tall and lush if left uncut through the summer, swamping any wildflowers. Cutting the area and removing the hay every year will slowly reduce the fertility of the soil, but this may take some time to be effective. In the meantime if this is the case in your garden, you may wish to cut earlier in the summer – perhaps at the end of June or during July. One other

Yellow rattle is a valuable meadow plant, reducing the vigour of grasses

thing you can do to curb the exuberant grasses is to establish a plant called **yellow rattle** an amazing annual wildflower that grows in ancient hay meadows. This semi-parasitic plant is able to reduce the height and vitality of the grasses by taking nourishment through their roots. The seeds of yellow rattle need to be sown onto short grass in the autumn - it is just about the only wildflower that can be sown in this way. It does not always establish first time, but it is worth persevering as it can make a great difference to the vigour of the grasses and thus the establishment of your wildflowers. Scatter the large seeds thinly after cutting and raking, trying where you can to ensure that they have reached the soil surface. With the right conditions they should germinate in the following spring.

56

What not to plant

As with all the other areas we have explored, there are certain wildflowers that are best left out of your grassy habitats. In general these include all the very vigorous plants that have already been mentioned, but especially hogweed and cow parsley. As useful as these are for attracting wildlife, they are best confined to a wild patch (see Chapter 9)if you would like to include them in your garden. It is probably best to restrict your choices to wildflowers that are specifically recommended for planting into lawns, as these will be species that are known to coexist happily with grasses.

What wildlife can you expect?

Grassy areas are brilliant for wildlife of all kinds for several reasons. Firstly, they are habitats that remain completely undisturbed for long periods throughout the spring and summer enabling a range of creatures, including small mammals and many species of insect, to set up home. Voles, shrews and wood mice can often be found in long grass, and hedgehogs will make their summer nests in undisturbed grass. Birds also enjoy meadow areas, as they can be a great source of food. Seeds from the wildflowers and grasses will provide sustenance, but many insect-eating birds will find the food they are seeking here. Hay meadows in the countryside are probably best known for their ability to support a wide range of butterflies and this can be true of the grassy places in our gardens also. Many beautiful species, including meadow brown, ringlet, marbled white and gatekeeper lay their eggs on meadow grasses and these are the plants on which their caterpillars feed. Some of these butterfly species may well establish themselves in grass and wildflower areas in a garden situation. In addition,

Ringlet butterflies often breed in garden meadows

many of the meadow flowers that have been mentioned are good nectar providers for butterflies, especially field scabious, greater knapweed and bird's foot trefoil. Long grass in your garden will enhance its wildlife attracting potential as well as provide you with an area that has colour and interest throughout the spring and summer.

Other plants suitable for grassy places

Plant name	Latin name	Flowering months	Height	Sowing time	Seed Treatment Cold	Scarify
Betony	Stachys officinalis	June - Aug	15-70 cms	Spring		
Bladder Campion	Silene vulgaris	May – Aug	25-100 cms	Spring		
Common Knapweed	Centaurea nigra	June – Sept	30-75 cms	Spring		
Lady's Bedstraw	Galium verum	July – Aug	20-100 cms	Spring		
Meadow Cranesbill	Geranium pratense	June – Aug	30-80 cms	Autumn	✓	✓
Mouse-ear Hawkweed	Hieracium pilosella	May – Sept	5-25 cms	Spring		
Rough Hawkbit	Leontodon hispidus	June – Aug	10-50 cms	Spring	✓	
Sheep's Sorrel	Rumex acetosella	May – July	10-25 cms	Spring		
Wild Basil	Clinopodium vulgare	July – Sept	10-40 cms	Spring		
Yarrow	Achillea millefolium	June - Sept	10-50 cms	Spring		

You could also try:

Autumn hawkbit, bird's-eye primrose, bird's foot trefoil, common sorrel, daisy, devil's-bit scabious, dog violet, dropwort, goat's beard, hedge bedstraw, lady's smock, meadow buttercup, meadowsweet, meadow vetchling, musk mallow, primrose, quaking grass, ragged robin, red clover, salad burnet, selfheal, snakeshead fritillary, sneezewort, St. John's wort, sweet violet, tufted vetch, wild daffodil, wild carrot, wild marjoram.

Gatekeeper butterflies love the nectar from wild marjoram flowers

STAR PLANTS FOR GRASSY PLACES

Field Scabious
Knautia arvensis

One of the best wildflowers for late summer nectar, especially for bumblebees and butterflies. Mauve flowers on strong stems, which carry on well into September in good weather. The seed germinates easily but sporadically in spring. Also suitable for a sunny border. Height 40-100 cms.

Cowslip
Primula veris

One of our most beautiful wildflowers, the cowslip produces its sweetly scented yellow flowers in April and May. It grows in almost any type of grass and once established will self seed easily. Seeds can also be sown into pots in the autumn and left outside until spring when they will germinate readily. Also suitable for damp places and light shade. Height 10-35 cms.

Hoary Plantain
Plantago media

An unusual and interesting flower, the hoary plantain has fluffy pink flower spikes from May all through the summer. Small insects are attracted to the pollen. Seeds should be sown in spring and germinate easily but sporadically. Also suitable for a sunny border. Height 15-25 cms.

Greater Knapweed
Centaurea scabiosa

An excellent plant for this habitat having strong upright flowers which attract many butterfly species and bumblebees plus goldfinches to the ripened seeds. Seed germinates in spring with no pre-treatment. Also suitable for a sunny border. Height 30-80 cms.

Yellow Rattle
Rhinanthus minor

Just about the only annual wildflower that will survive in grass, this pretty, yellow semi-parasitic flower suppresses vigorous grass. Seeds should be sown in the autumn directly onto grass that has been cut and thoroughly raked. The flowers attract bees. Height 10-20 cms.

Oxeye Daisy
Leucanthemum vulgare

This familiar white wildflower can be seen on roadsides and in verges en masse in May and June. It attracts bees and some butterflies to its nectar. The seeds germinate easily in the spring with no pre-treatment. Also suitable for light shade. Height 30-100 cms.

CHAPTER 7
WILD CLIMBERS AND SCRAMBLERS

In the British Isles we have a great number of really attractive herbaceous wildflowers suitable for almost any garden situation, but our numbers of climbing (or scrambling) plants are rather fewer. However, there is still a good selection for the wildflower enthusiast, both of flowering species and those that are grown mainly for their foliage. Ivy, **hops**, **honeysuckle** and the wild roses in particular have attractive leaves and fragrant flowers and are suitable for covering walls, fences or garden sheds, and ivy has the added advantage of being evergreen. In addition, this group of plants will encourage a wide range of wildlife to your garden.

Suitable spots for wild climbers

In nature these scrambling and climbing plants tend to grow into hedgerows or through trees where light levels are low. This means that most of our wild climbers are suitable for more shady places in the garden making them particularly valuable, although most will adapt to more sunny positions. Ivy can quickly cover a north-facing wall where little else will grow, and wild honeysuckle can be encouraged to grow up a trellis fixed to the shady side of a fence, but both will happily cope with lighter, sunnier conditions. Soil must also be considered, especially in north-facing places or alongside south-facing walls and fences. These challenging spots can often be dry and lacking in nutrients. Whenever a native climber or scrambler is grown, it is important to make sure it is planted with all the care and attention you would give to a flowering clematis or rambling rose. Well-rotted compost into the planting hole, and a mulch of compost or bark on the surface to conserve water are both essential. Watering after planting and throughout the first summer will help your climber to establish well in what could be a very dry spot.

Enhancing hedges and shrubs

If you are fortunate enough to have a wild hedge of native shrubs on your garden boundary, it will probably be full of hawthorn and blackthorn flowers in the spring, and sparkling with red and black berries in the autumn and winter. Sadly, the ubiquitous privet hedge can be very boring indeed and benefits greatly from the flowers and foliage of a few native climbers and scramblers, which are adapted to just these sorts of conditions in the wild. However climbers and scramblers should only be added to a well-established hedge or group of shrubs. Honeysuckle, hops and wild roses can grow quite rapidly and may swamp small hedge plants that do not yet have good root systems. It is worth remembering if you are planning to plant a new hedge, that it is best not to add any scrambling plants such as **dog rose** or honeysuckle until the second or third year after planting when the shrubs themselves are well established.

Wild ramblers in hedges look wonderful and add a huge amount of extra interest. Honeysuckle in particular has the ability to find its way through the hedge foliage and emerge at the top, where its sweetly perfumed blossoms will scent the evening air. **Traveller's joy** (also called old man's beard) will also thrive in this situation, but prefers a soil rich in lime.

The feathery seedheads of traveller's joy catch the autumn light

The wild roses (sweet briar and dog rose) are vigorous, prickly climbers, and will fill a boring hedge with powder pink fragrant roses in early summer. Sweet briar is especially attractive as both the flowers and the leaves are scented. In light rain the air around this climber is perfumed with the sweet smell of apples. Both dog rose and sweet briar have the familiar pink open flowers and both species attract many insects. The flowers are followed in the autumn by bright red hips – winter food for many birds including thrushes and blackbirds and for a few small mammal species especially wood mice. These wild roses need to be cut down to ground level every few years to ensure that they produce fresh young foliage and plenty of flowers. Being rapid growers means that without this occasional maintenance, they become dominated by thick, bare and very prickly stems.

Another good choice of climber for enhancing a bland hedge is the narrow-leaved everlasting pea, a native relative of the sweet pea. The unscented flowers are a dark, dusky pink and are produced profusely on clinging stems which reach up to 2 meters. Lower down at the base of a hedgerow, some of the species of vetch will happily make their home. **Tufted vetch** and wood vetch will both scramble through vegetation along the bottom of a hedge or into low shrubs. Both have the delicate foliage we associate with this family of plants, but tufted vetch is the commoner of the two species in the wild. Its bright purple clusters of small flowers can often be seen along roadsides, in meadows or at the base of a hedge and it flowers late into the summer. In the garden it will climb to a height of a metre or more and is a useful wildflower for covering unsightly low fencing. Wood vetch has larger, paler flowers with dark purple veins. This plant will scramble to a height of 2 metres or more.

If you don't have hedges around your garden, these plants can still be grown through ornamental shrubs if you wish. Plant them sparingly as they will spread of their own accord. All can be cut back hard as necessary to make sure that the shrubs are not swamped.

Pergolas, archways and wigwams

Wooden structures in gardens are becoming ever more popular, but not every gardener wants the inevitable clematis to adorn their pergola, lovely as many of the species and hybrids of this plant are. Our native climbers are very wildlife friendly, making good nest sites, and an archway or pergola can provide a safe nesting place for a robin or blackbird when covered with a tangle of hops or traveller's joy. The wild hop has separate male and female plants so try to make sure you obtain a female plant – this will bear the attractive light green hops which can be picked and dried for display inside the house (or used to make beer!) A hop will spread very quickly, both as it scrambles and climbs, and underground, so plant with care. Hops look very attractive covering a long pergola and are also suitable to twine over an unsightly shed, or along a larchlap fence. Bear in mind that if planted along a fence they are likely to pop up on the other side, so think carefully about your neighbours before planting this exuberant climber. Also suitable for covering sheds or fences is the traveller's joy or old man's beard. Its fluffy seed heads add interest to the winter garden and the tiny spring flowers, although not terribly conspicuous, are very sweetly scented. This plant, like the hop, can also be an enthusiastic spreader, but is easily controlled by cutting back in late winter.

This archway is covered with the golden variety of our wild hop

Wigwams and archways are excellent supports for wild honeysuckle, perhaps combined with the narrow-leaved everlasting pea, but are less suitable for the more vigorous climbers. The vetches too would scramble into the lower reaches of a willow or hazel support or along the bottom of a trellis fence, providing a welcome splash of long-lasting purple flowers. Lastly the yellow **meadow vetchling** is a similar plant to the tufted vetch, with curling leafy tendrils that cling to grass stalks. This plant has bright yellow clusters of pea type flowers and can be used to scramble into the lower reaches of other climbers such as honeysuckle, especially in more sunny spots.

Ivy – to grow or not to grow?

If attracting wildlife to your garden is a priority then ivy is an important native climber to include. It has many advantages as it covers unsightly features quickly and provides food for many species of native wildlife. Being evergreen it has excellent nest sites and shelter for hibernating creatures. Ivy is an enthusiastic climber and needs to be grown with care on house walls but in wilder parts of the garden it can be left on the ground to provide ground cover or allowed to climb boundary walls. It is often thought that ivy should be

Stunning in its simplicity - the wild dog rose

prevented from growing into trees, as it can cause instability or can 'strangle' trees. This is not the case – a tree will only suffer from a growth of ivy high in its branches if it is already diseased or dead. Ivy is one of the most useful wildlife plants we can grow in our gardens, but you may decide that keeping it under control would be too much work for you.

What not to plant

As our choice of native climbers and scramblers is rather limited, so is the number that we should avoid in our gardens. Hedge bindweed has wonderful white trumpet-shaped flowers and spreads like wildfire, tangling its twining stems around anything it comes across, but I know several people who cultivate it and its naturally occurring pink form which is beautiful. Goose grass however, has little to recommend it and should be avoided. Woody nightshade is an attractive plant with small exotic looking flowers followed by bright scarlet berries. Sadly the berries are poisonous so this scrambler is best avoided for that reason only. Lastly the white bryony, again a lovely climber for a hedge, has poisonous yellow and orange berries.

What wildlife can you expect?

Native climbers, if chosen and planted with care, can enhance the wildlife value of a garden tremendously. They can provide food for insects in the form of nectar and pollen and many have berries or seeds which birds and small mammals will eat. Their great value however comes in their growth habit – tangles of vegetation that can be used by many species of bird for nesting and for shelter. A thick climber such as traveller's joy growing against a wall will create

Red admiral butterflies will feast on the nectar they find in autumn ivy flowers

a warm, dry and safe place for a thrush to build a nest, or ivy with its evergreen leaves will encourage a dunnock to make a home. A thicket of ivy is also a useful hibernation place for butterflies, especially brimstones seeking a frost-free place to spend the winter. Indeed, their wings are thought to be shaped like an ivy leaf, which increases the camouflage. Ivy also has nectar and pollen for many insects including red admiral butterflies late in the summer, and its crop of juicy berries appear late in the winter when almost all natural food for birds has disappeared. In all, our climbers play a very important part in the garden habitat, both feeding and sheltering wildlife and adding colour and interest to dull hedges and walls.

Bumblebees may 'steal' nectar from tufted vetch by making a hole at the base of the flower

Other suitable climbing or scrambling wildflowers

Plant name	Latin name	Flowering months	Height	Sowing time	Seed Treatment	
					Cold	Scarify
Field Bindweed	Convolvulus arvensis	June – Sept	100-200 cms	Spring		
Hedge Bedstraw	Galium mollugo	May – Sept	50-100 cms	Spring		
Hedge Bindweed	Calystegia sepium	June – Sept	100-300 cms	Spring		
Ivy	Hedera helix	Sept - Nov	1-30 m	Autumn	✓	
Ivy-leaved Toadflax	Cymbalaria muralis	May - Sept	10-60 cms	Spring		
Narrow-leaved Pea	Lathyrus sylvestris	June - Aug	1-3 m	Spring		✓
Sea Pea	Lathyrus japonicus	June – Aug	50-100 cms	Spring		✓
Sweet Briar	Rosa rubiginosa	June - July	1-3 m	Autumn	✓	
Wood Vetch	Vicia sylvatica	June – Aug	1-2 m	Spring		✓
Yellow Vetchling	Lathyrus aphaca	June – Aug	30-50 cms	Spring		✓

You could also try:

Bittersweet, black bryony, bramble, greater stitchwort, lady's bedstraw, white bryony, wild madder.

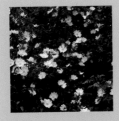

Dog Rose
Rosa canina

This scrambling rose typifies early summer in the countryside, with its sweetly scented pale pink flowers. This is an easy climber to grow in sun or light shade. Seed germinate only slowly and if sown in the autumn it may take more than one winter to break dormancy. The flowers attract bees and hoverflies in June and July. Height up to 3 m.

Tufted Vetch
Vicia cracca

A gorgeous scrambling plant that looks wonderful at the base of a hedge. The spikes of bright purple flowers appear in late summer, through into September. They attract bumblebees. The seeds should be scarified and sown in early spring. Also suitable for a meadow. Height 50-100 cms.

Wild Hop
Humulus lupulus

This is a vigorous plant and should only be planted where there is plenty of space for rambling. A female plant will produce the pretty 'cones' in late summer. Larval food plant of the comma butterfly and good cover for nesting birds. Sow seeds outside in autumn. Height up to 5 or 6 m.

Meadow Vetchling
Lathyrus pratensis

This yellow flowered vetch is a delightful plant, rambling through long grass at the base of a hedge and attracting a range of insects, but especially bees, from May through the summer. Seed should be scarified before sowing in spring. Also suitable for a meadow. Height 30-100 cms.

Wild Honeysuckle
Lonicera periclymenum

A climber that needs no introduction. Wild honeysuckle will scramble beautifully through a hedge or up a pergola or fence. Scented moth-attracting flowers in June and July are followed by red berries which birds relish. Sow the berries in autumn. Height up to 5 m.

Traveller's Joy
Clematis vitalba

Also called old man's beard, this is a very vigorous climber. The small white flowers in July are followed by fluffy seedheads. A good nesting plant for birds, and the flowers attract bees. Seeds should be sown outside in the autumn. Height up to 20 m

CHAPTER 8
WILDFLOWERS FOR CONTAINERS, WINDOW BOXES AND SMALL GARDENS

Anyone with a small garden, or perhaps no garden at all, need not feel left out when it comes to cultivating our native flowers. In the wild there are many attractive species that are adapted to growing in relatively inhospitable habitats including scree slopes where the soil is thin and poor or on dry chalky banks. Some of these plants are true alpines, and can often be found in the alpine section of any garden centre. These and other small species are able to adapt to living in containers where space is tight. Add to this group some of the tiny plants of chalk grassland slopes, or small species that may inhabit cracks in walls and rocks, and you will see that there is plenty of choice if you have a small garden, a patio with containers, or simply a window box.

Choose plants for your conditions

As with each of the sections in this book so far we first have to look at the local conditions in our immediate environment. In containers we have less of a problem with type of soil or how much water our plants may need as these are conditions we can change. If the plants we are choosing are found in the wild on the sides of mountains or on dry chalky soil we must use appropriate compost – one with plenty of grit to provide the drainage these plants require. If a few wild bog plants are more to your taste, the soil and drainage in a container can be adapted for these types of plants and there is more information on making a mini bog garden on page 46. The only factors that need to be taken into account are those of light and shade and hopefully containers can be positioned appropriately. However, if you have a small garden or patio which is north facing and receives little direct sunlight, you will need to choose your plants with care.

Using containers

Almost any type of container can be used for growing wildflowers, from wooden half barrels or old stone sinks to beautiful Mediterranean style glazed pots. The container itself is not important, but compost, drainage and watering are. As the majority of the small wildflowers that are suitable for container growing require good drainage, a soil based compost with extra grit is a good choice, plus the container must have good drainage holes. Many container composts are based on peat, which should be avoided at all costs. Apart from the damage that peat extraction causes in fragile wetland habitats, peat composts hold lots of water, which is something we do not need here. A layer of large gravel or broken terracotta pot pieces to increase drainage should be placed at the bottom of the container. Cover this layer with your compost to within a few centimeters of the surface of the pot and firm it gently. After planting your chosen species, the surface of the container can be mulched with small stones or grit, but this is by no means essential.

In general, watering should be thorough but infrequent. Water well when the container is dry and allow it to drain thoroughly. Usually, natural rainfall will take care of the watering for you, so simply be aware of the weather conditions and check occasionally that your containers have not dried out severely.

Many small wildflowers are suitable for growing in this way. Their sizes vary so check their heights on pages 74 and 75 to give you an idea of which are suitable for the smallest spaces and which require rather more room. For the smallest pot or window box, pink-flowered wild thyme, yellow stonecrop or **rockrose, heartsease** and pale blue harebell would make a stunning combination of varying colours and shapes. These would all require a sunny position. Other small wildflowers suitable for containers are the delicate meadow saxifrage

These harebells fill a wild bank with blooms, but will adapt readily to a small garden

with its clusters of surprisingly large white flowers, alpine lady's mantle with tiny green flowers and lovely foliage, and mountain avens which has white flowers and crinkled evergreen leaves. Plants requiring a little more space include **small scabious** with mauve flowers which attract butterflies, the fantastic **wild marjoram**, two bright yellow trefoils - **bird's foot trefoil** and horseshoe vetch, delicate quaking grass which graces our limestone hills and chalky meadows, and bloody cranesbill, a useful shade tolerant plant with open purple flowers.

Wildflowers for cracks in paving and walls

As we have seen, many of the plants that are suitable for growing in small spaces come from rocky habitats or even the sea shore, which means that some of them are ideal for planting in pockets of soil along the tops of walls or in between paving. The bright yellow wild rockrose. white sea campion, mauve sheep's bit and ivy-leaved toadflax which has tiny snapdragon like flowers, are all suitable for planting in this way. Perhaps the most obvious species is the creeping thyme which will spread out beautifully over paving and seed into new spaces. A few species, especially the yellow stonecrop, which is also known as wall pepper, will grow on a tiled roof. It found its way onto the roof of my last house

Sheep's bit will grow in dry conditions on walls or between paving stones

and I loved the bright splash of yellow up there in late spring, but it had a habit of blocking the guttering! However, folklore says that it protects a house from lightning so I was happy to leave it. This and several other species are extremely drought tolerant, making them more able to withstand the difficult conditions of heat and drought that dominate the tops of walls or around paving. When planting into these small spaces, try to make sure that there is sufficient soil around the plants' roots. Although these species will survive in what may seem like no soil at all, they first need to establish a root system. Make sure they are watered frequently after planting until new shoots are appearing. It is not an easy task to establish plants in these dry and inhospitable places and you may need to try several times, but once they are happy they will generally seed and spread freely of their own accord.

Mini meadows and cornfields

If you long for a touch of the countryside in your patio garden you may be tempted to try a tiny meadow or area of cornfield flowers in a large container. This can work, but only with a fair degree of planning. The crucial thing is to have soil as poor in nutrients as possible – it could be from a dry, dusty corner of the garden somewhere, or perhaps from a hole where a pond is to be established. Garden soil of reasonable fertility or garden centre compost will not be suitable. The aim in using poor soil is to stunt the growth of your meadow grasses or cornfield flowers to prevent them flopping out of the sides of your container.

Cornfield annuals can be sown directly into a large container using the method described

Mountain avens has delicate white flowers, evergreen foliage and a creeping habit

on page 21. The container should be placed in full sun and watered occasionally until the seed germinates. A mini meadow can also be sown in a similar way. Push the seeds into the levelled soil, but leave them uncovered. It is even more essential to obtain nutrient-poor soil for a project such as this as the meadow grasses will become tall and leggy, overpowering the wildflowers if the soil has more than the minimum amount of nutrients. Your choice of seeds is also important here. A mixture of meadow wildflowers and grasses for a chalky soil is more likely to succeed, as these species tend to be shorter. Seed suppliers listed on page 91 will be able to advise you on your choice of seeds.

Another option is to sow an informal wildflower container by using a mixture of seeds, without grasses. Sea campion, small scabious, heartsease, and bird's foot trefoil will grow easily from seed and create an attractive mixture of colourful native flowers. Alternatively, single terracotta pots with one species per pot can look stunning and if chosen carefully can bring butterflies and bees to your back door. Wild marjoram, wild rockrose, clustered bellflower and restharrow, all look lovely grown in this way and if placed in a sunny position attract a variety of butterfly species and bumblebees to their flowers.

Climbers in containers

Some of the climbers mentioned in Chapter 7 can be established in containers, to be trained over trellis or up walls in a tiny garden. Most suitable are the smaller species, in particular the narrow leaved everlasting pea, tufted vetch, wood vetch and meadow vetchling. Some of the others are rather too vigorous for container growth, but wild honeysuckle does well in a pot especially if nutrients are added, and it will reach a good height. With a smaller scrambler such as wood vetch amongst its lower stems, it can look very attractive indeed, and will encourage the wonderful hawk moths to its nectar.

Caring for your small wildflowers over time

Containers are often seen as rather transitory collections of plants, where bulbs and bedding are removed and replaced at regular intervals. This does not need to be the case, and with perennial wildflowers, there is no reason at all why they cannot remain in their pots for some time. They are economical in terms of their nutrient usage and will grow happily in the same pot for many seasons. Some will self-seed (heartsease in particular is short lived but replaces itself very regularly). A minimum amount of maintenance will be needed to make sure that your wildflower containers continue to look good. If growth over time is very slow, a small amount of compost added as a mulch will help, but don't overdo it or the plants may well outgrow their containers. Plants may occasionally need replacing, or you may wish to try new species or combinations. Other than that, it is simply a case of a little gentle tidying late in the winter or early spring, cutting back dead stems after the seeds have gone to allow the new season's growth to emerge. It is best not to do this too early in the year, as young growth can be damaged by late frosts, and beneficial insects such as ladybirds, tucked inside dead hollow stems may get a rude awakening from their hibernation. Compost your clippings, but otherwise enjoy an almost maintenance free small garden!

Pasque flower is now rare in the wild but is often grown in gardens

Plants in paving and walls may also need a little tidying as outlined above. Again it is best to do this after seeds have fallen as you will want your wildflowers to spread into corners and cracks. Most will do this without assistance if seeds are allowed to ripen and fall of their own accord. However, the seeds of **pasque flower** are best collected as soon as they are dry and sown immediately into pots if you wish to increase your stocks of this lovely wildflower. Other than these easy tasks wild thyme and wild heather both benefit from the occasional clipping with a pair of garden shears or strong scissors.

What not to plant

It stands to reason that the plants to avoid in small gardens are those that are rampant growers. Restrict yourself to the plants that are recommended and you won't go far wrong. Plants that seed very freely are also best left out of containers, window boxes or small beds. These are likely to be the species that could make a nuisance of themselves in gaps in paving.

What wildlife can you expect?

Many of the small wildflowers mentioned are good nectar and pollen providers for

honeybees, bumblebees, hoverflies and butterflies. Wild marjoram is one of the best nectar providers for the smaller butterfly species, small scabious and thyme are loved by small tortoiseshell butterflies and the vetches are very attractive to bumblebees. Bird's foot trefoil not only attracts the common blue butterfly to its flowers, but this species also lays its eggs on the leaves of the plant. Growing bird's foot trefoil in a container or window box may even encourage this pretty butterfly to establish a breeding colony in your tiny garden.

The burnet moths use bird's foot trefoil as a food plant for their caterpillars

Other suitable wildflowers for containers, window boxes and small gardens

Plant name	Latin name	Flowering months	Height	Sowing time	Seed Treatment	
					Cold	Scarify
Alpine Lady's Mantle	Alchemilla alpina	June – Aug	5-10 cms	Autumn	✓	
Bloody Cranesbill	Geranium sanguineum	July – Aug	10-35 cms	Autumn		✓
Harebell	Campanula rotundifolia	July – Sept	10-30 cms	Spring		
Horseshoe Vetch	Hippocrepis comosa	May – Aug	10-20 cms	Spring		✓
Lily Of The Valley	Convallaria majalis	May – June	15-25 cms	Use rhizomes		
Meadow Saxifrage	Saxifraga granulata	Apr – June	10-25 cms	Spring		
Mountain Avens	Dryas octapetala	May – July	3-7 cms	Spring		
Quaking Grass	Briza media	June – Aug	20-40 cms	Spring		
Wild Thyme	Thymus drucei	June – July	2-6 cms	Spring		
Yellow Stonecrop	Sedum acre	June - July	2-6 cms	Autumn		

You could also try:

Basil thyme, birds eye primrose, bugle, clustered bellflower, common centaury, common toadflax, cowslip, creeping Jenny, daisy, dog violet, English stonecrop, ground ivy, ivy-leaved toadflax, lady's bedstraw, lesser celandine, maiden pink, meadow vetchling, mountain pansy, mouse-ear hawkweed, narrow leaved everlasting pea, perennial flax, primrose, purple saxifrage, restharrow, rock cinquefoil, scarlet pimpernel, sea campion, selfheal, sheep's bit, silverweed, sweet violet, thrift, tufted vetch, Welsh poppy, wild daffodil, wild heather, wild strawberry, wood vetch.

Wild Rockrose — Helianthemum nummularium

This is a stunning little wildflower – in reality a tiny shrub – with masses of bright yellow flowers in early summer. A larval food plant of the green hairstreak and brown argus butterflies plus nectar for bees. Slow and sporadic germination although scarification can help. Also suitable for sunny borders. Height 5-25 cms.

Pasque Flower — Pulsatilla vulgaris

Perhaps one of the most stunning of our native flowers. The bright purple petals with their central boss of yellow stamens attract early bees from April until June. The fluffy seeds germinate easily if sown when really fresh. Height 10-20 cms.

Wild Marjoram — Origanum vulgare

This wildflower is worth its weight in gold. Bees and butterflies, especially gatekeepers, common blues and small tortoiseshells love it and you can eat the leaves too! Late summer flowering, it provides nectar from July to the end of the summer. Tiny seeds should be sown in spring and not covered. Also suitable for a meadow or sunny border. Height 20-40 cms.

Heartease — Viola tricolor

A sweet little colourful flower, sometimes annual but often lasting a second year. Will self-seed, so easy to keep going. The flower colour varies although is usually some combination of yellow, purple and mauve with dark insect-attracting guide lines. Heartsease can flower at almost any time from spring until autumn. Also suitable for a sunny border. Height 5-20 cms.

Small Scabious — Scabiosa columbaria

The small scabious is perfect for those spots where the field scabious is too large and boisterous. This more dainty plant has mauve flowers that attract many insects especially butterflies and bees, and it flowers profusely from mid to late summer. The seed germinates easily if sown in spring and gently pressed into the compost. Also suitable for the front of a sunny border. Height 15-30 cms.

Bird's Foot Trefoil — Lotus corniculatus

Masses of bright yellow and orange flowers, the larval food plant of the common blue butterfly, nectar for bees and butterflies – this is a well behaved, useful and very pretty wildflower for pots, window boxes, gravel gardens and sunny borders. The seed should be scarified before sowing in spring. Also suitable for a meadow. Height 10-25 cms.

CHAPTER 9
A WILD PLACE FOR WILDLIFE

Every plant has its place

Throughout this book there have been lists of wildflowers to avoid in certain situations in our gardens – there are plenty of native flowers that could be considered unsuitable for cultivation, especially in smaller gardens. There are others that, to some eyes, are not attractive enough to earn a place in a border or around a paved sitting area. Sadly some of these plants are the very best at attracting wildlife, so if a wildlife friendly garden is your aim, you may be missing out on some opportunities to support your local wildlife. The purpose of this chapter is to suggest a way in which some of these wildflowers can be grown without compromising the rest of the garden. If attracting wildlife is not your main aim, or the idea of an 'untidy' patch does not appeal to you, then this chapter is not necessarily for you, but I would still urge you to think about the idea of leaving a small area in your garden undisturbed. You may find that the extra wildlife that visits you will stimulate your interest, and you will soon develop a sense of satisfaction that you are doing something very positive for the wildlife in your area. You may even be persuaded by the idea that a hedgehog might take up residence in your wild patch, and come to appreciate the benefits of having a resident pest controller!

Designating a wild patch

A garden area that is left undisturbed need not be enormous – in fact even just a few square metres will provide a refuge for hibernating ladybirds in the winter, create a feeding place for small mammals such as shrews (which are avid slug devourers) and make a space for a bumblebee to create a nest. Perhaps the most useful way in which to start a wild patch is to place a few logs in a shady place where the grass can be left to grow long. This could be alongside a hedge or some dense shrubs. The wood will slowly break down and provide food for many invertebrates including woodlice or the larvae of beetles. These creatures in turn will attract birds and small mammals, including hedgehogs, which will be searching your garden for food. A small community of animals will quickly build up around this little habitat. Once your area is decided upon, you can start to add appropriate wildflowers. A must is the **white deadnettle** – a really attractive wildflower but prone to spread and wander in borders. Here it would be no trouble and indeed a great asset. Flowering early, perhaps even in February if the weather is very mild, it is a favourite pollen source for bumblebees. **Dandelions** too could be allowed to flourish here. They provide early nectar for the first butterflies, especially the peacock, when they emerge from hibernation, plus seeds for goldfinches.

The grasses around your wild patch, if allowed to flower and grow tall, do not only provide

77

cover and shelter for wildlife. They are also food for a range of insects including the caterpillars of some moths and butterflies, so you may help to increase the local population of these species. Insects that feed on the grasses in turn will attract birds, hedgehogs, bats and even foxes.

If you are able to dedicate a larger space to your undisturbed patch, a great variety of useful plants is available to you. Some of our most attractive native species can be a little too invasive in the main garden area. **Rosebay willowherb** is a perfect example – tall spikes of deep pink flowers attracting moths to their nectar and providing food for the caterpillar of the fabulous elephant hawk moth. However, this plant is rampant, and should only be grown where its flamboyant nature will not be a problem. Other wildflowers that could be included in a larger wild area are the familiar creeping buttercup, the cheerful bright yellow lesser celandine, and the stately **teasel**, a wildflower that attracts a huge range of wildlife including butterflies, bumblebees and goldfinches, the latter enjoying the teasel's seeds through the winter months.

Humble buttercups can light up a grassy patch

There are more possibilities if you are happy with the prospect of plants doing their own thing. Cow parsley has wonderful frothy white flowers in May, hogweed attracts masses of hoverflies, and woody nightshade, if you are certain that the berries are safe from visitors to your garden, will ramble and clamber over logs, twig piles and hedge plants. This may also be a place where you would be happier with the idea of growing ivy, maybe as ground cover, although grown in this way it will not produce the useful nectar-producing flowers and the berries which do so much to feed some of our birds in the late winter.

Of course you do not need to restrict yourself to wildflowers that are rampant or undesirable in other parts of your garden. Foxgloves, vetches, field scabious, knapweed, moon daisies and red and white campions are all robust enough to hold their own in slightly wilder conditions. In shadier spots hedge woundwort is another good choice along with greater stitchwort, St John's wort and herb Robert. The possibilities are

The yellow flowers of wild parsnip will bring hoverflies to a wild patch

endless. A key point in an area such as this, if attracting wildlife is a priority, is that it is disturbed as little as possible.

Growing a few 'weeds'

Nettles, thistles and **brambles** together with some of the species already mentioned in this chapter including dandelions and hogweed, are all considered to be 'weeds' by the average gardener. To the wildflower gardener they are simply rather over enthusiastic plants, and, if you have room for them, deserve a place in your wild patch. Nettles play an important part in the life cycles of several of our native butterflies, providing leaves upon which the caterpillars feed, so this is a good plant to include if you have the space. You should be aware though, that the red admiral, small tortoiseshell, painted lady, peacock and comma butterflies, all of which will use this plant as a larval food plant, are really only likely to use the nettles for breeding if the plants are in full sunlight. If your wild patch is in the shade, forget about the nettles and plant foxgloves instead. Thistles and brambles will grow in a more shady spot and both are excellent wildlife attracting species, having nectar for butterflies and bees. Brambles also provide good,

Nettles are vital to the survival of several of our native butterfly species

safe shelter for nesting birds and small mammals, and berries for you or your visiting wildlife.

Looking after your wild patch

By its very nature a wild patch will become untidy and overgrown, but this is really the point. To attract wildlife it is best if there is as little disturbance as possible which means that maintenance work in this area will be minimal. The wilder part of my previous garden was the place where I was most likely to see the greatest variety of interesting creatures, from red admiral butterflies and grass snakes, to green woodpeckers and roe deer. It was always a delightful area to visit at any time of year, and somewhere that I always felt comfortable, partly because I was able to sit and enjoy my time there, without feeling that I should be busy doing something! The design of my new garden incorporates many wilder areas where there will be little to do except some annual maintenance, to ensure that the area does not disappear completely under a tangle of brambles. In any area such as this, grasses, nettles and wildflower stems should be cut down to about 20 centimetres in late winter, preferably using a hand sickle or hook. Take care that you are not disturbing a hibernating hedgehog. The cuttings can be gently raked up and placed on a compost heap, or left in a pile somewhere to provide a habitat for creatures such as slow worms. This annual cutting will allow the wildflowers to seed and spread and prevent them from becoming lost under the more rampant grasses. If you have brambles or ivy you may wish to cut these back at this time. Bramble stems will arch and root at their tips, making them very effective colonisers of bare space round about them. Cut back any stray stems to the main bush and dig up any rooted tips. This done annually should keep them under control. Little else remains to be done except perhaps to add more logs to your log pile if you have one, to replace those that have decayed.

What wildlife can you expect?

Some of the wildlife that may visit a wild patch in your garden has already been mentioned. But in fact there is practically no limit to the kinds of creatures that may be attracted to an area such as this. The invertebrates that will take up residence here will attract a wide range of other creatures. Mammals, birds, reptiles, amphibians and other insects will come looking for food. Bumblebees may make their nests, toads might hibernate in the log piles, peacock butterflies lay their eggs on the sunny nettles, wrens nest in the brambles and hedgehogs breed in the long grass. The fact that an area such as this could also be full of dandelions, foxgloves, cow parsley and willowherb, making it colourful and exuberant, is an added bonus.

Even if wildlife isn't a priority in your garden you can still add a wild patch if you wish, and plant a selection of wildflowers. Allow them to spread and seed as they will, making a natural area - your own tiny piece of countryside.

A shady seat in your wild patch will encourage you to relax and enjoy the wildlife

A red admiral butterfly takes shelter in a hogweed seedhead

Other plants suitable for wild places

Plant name	Latin name	Flowering months	Height	Sowing time	Seed Treatment	
					Cold	Scarify
Common Toadflax	Linaria vulgaris	July – Oct	30-60 cms	Spring		
Cow Parsley	Anthriscus sylvestris	April – June	60-150 cms	Autumn	✓	
Ground Ivy	Glechoma hederacea	Mar - June	10-20 cms	Spring		
Hedge Woundwort	Stachys sylvatica	June – Sept	40-80 cms	Autumn		
Meadow Buttercup	Ranunculus acris	May – Aug	12-40 cms	Spring		
Red Clover	Trifolium pratense	May – July	10-20 cms	Spring		✓
Selfheal	Prunella vulgaris	May- Oct	5-20 cms	Spring		
Tansy	Tanacetum vulgare	July – Sept	30-120 cms	Spring		
Wild Parsnip	Pastinaca sativa	June – Aug	30-120 cms	Autumn	✓	
Woolly Thistle	Circium eriophorum	July – Sept	100-150 cms	Spring		

You could also try:

Common comfrey, common knapweed, common sorrel, common thistle, field scabious, foxglove, goat's-beard, greater stitchwort, hedge bindweed, herb Robert, hogweed, hop, ivy, lesser celandine, lords and ladies, creeping buttercup, native grasses, oxeye daisy, red campion, red deadnettle, rough hawkbit, St John's wort, travellers joy, tufted vetch, white campion, wood avens, woody nightshade, yarrow.

Teasel   Dipsacus fullonum

Teasel is a rather spiny biennial plant with large spiky heads containing masses of tiny pink flowers through the summer. These attract insects including butterflies, bumblebees and hoverflies. Goldfinches flock to this plant once the seeds have set. Easy to grow from spring-sown seed and will self-seed once established. Also suitable for light shade. Height 100-200 cms.

White Deadnettle   Lamium album

White deadnettle is a creeping, spreading plant with light green leaves and whorls of hooded white flowers from May until October. Bumblebees absolutely love it so it is worth growing for this fact alone. Grows easily from seed sown in spring, or from dividing the spreading roots. Also suitable for light shade. Height 15-30 cms.

Bramble   Rubus fruticosus

Brambles come in all shapes and sizes, as it is a plant with many subspecies. All have pale pink or white flowers in early summer which attract bees and some butterflies, and blackberries which birds and mammals love. It is the dense tangle of prickly stems that make it especially good in a wild patch, providing shelter and nest sites. Seed should be sown in autumn and left outside. Also suitable as a climber. Height 100-200cms.

Dandelion   Taraxacum officinale

Bright yellow flowers throughout spring and summer, pretty fluffy seedheads and edible leaves – the dandelion is a very useful plant! Attracts a great range of wildlife including butterflies, bees and seed eating birds such as finches and linnets. Sow seed in spring, but this plant self seeds easily. Also suitable for a meadow. Height 5-30 cms.

Rosebay Willowherb   Chamaenerion angustifolium

This is a stunning, but rampant plant spreading both by seed and underground runners so only contemplate it if you have plenty of space and tolerance! It has tall spires of gorgeous rose pink flowers in summer from June to September, followed by attractive fluffy seedheads. The elephant hawkmoth caterpillar feeds on the leaves of this plant and bees collect the pollen and nectar. Sow seeds in autumn. Height 150-200 cms.

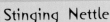

Stinging Nettle   Urtica dioica

A very familiar plant and one that is well known for its wildlife value. Only worth planting in a sheltered sunny spot if you want to attract butterflies, although other insects will use it and some birds will take the seeds in more shady places. The green flowers appear from June to late summer. Sow seed or transplant small self-sown plants in spring. Height 60-150 cms.

CHAPTER 10
LOOKING AFTER YOUR WILDFLOWER GARDEN

If, after reading this book, you have been inspired to grow some wildflowers in your garden borders, on your patio or even in your window box, you might be wondering about looking after this rather different sort of garden. Throughout the various chapters, there have been tips about the maintenance of your wildflowers and this chapter summarises those hints with an easy reference section on a season by season basis, so you can quickly check and decide which jobs should be done at particular times of year. But all in all, looking after a wildflower garden, or a more conventional garden that contains a few wildflowers, is no different from any other sort of gardening except that if you want to encourage wildlife it helps to be a little laid back. And we all like the idea of a garden that looks after itself to a certain extent!

This cornfield patch is dominated by the bright corn marigold

In this wildlife garden, wildflowers mingle with cottage garden varieties alongside a meadow area

Just like more conventional garden plants, there will be some wildflowers that are difficult to grow; they may need to be coaxed into bloom, protected from marauding slugs or may be fussy about their soil and surroundings. There will be others that have an urge to rampage through a border spreading seedlings wherever they can – they are plants after all and every species and variety has its own 'personality'. Inevitably there will be plants that do brilliantly in my garden, but curl up their toes in yours. That is just part and parcel of gardening and to some extent makes it an exciting and tantalising pastime. Will this plant grow or not? Will it flower this year or next? The key to being a good gardener is to go with the flow, get to know your plants, and graciously accept defeat occasionally! Grow what you can, choose species and varieties that have a natural affinity with your growing conditions and most importantly, have fun and relax in your garden. For an added dimension and a sense of purpose encourage wildlife where you can and your garden will become your own personal nature reserve. Growing wildflowers helps you to regard your garden as an important part of its natural surroundings.

In general a more relaxed approach to maintenance is required. In particular, tidying the garden at certain times of year, but especially in the autumn, is detrimental to wildlife in general and some plants in particular. Nature leaves winter foliage on many species for a purpose – to protect new spring buds, to enable seeds in their seedpods to experience winter frosts and provide a place for wildlife to find winter shelter. By removing this foliage and 'tidying up' we expose vulnerable wildlife, remove natural food and risk frost damage on new young shoots. Resist the temptation to tidy too much and enjoy winter frost on seedheads and bare stems. It will add a new dimension to your winter garden.

The next few pages have a summary of seasonal maintenance tasks, which should keep your wildflowers flourishing whether you have a single tub, a wildflower border or your whole garden is full of our native treasures. Whatever you decide to grow, looking after your wildflowers couldn't be easier.

SPRING

♦ In early spring you can begin to tidy herbaceous borders containing both wildflowers and non natives by removing last year's dead foliage. Take care not to disturb new shoots.

♦ Sow wildflower seeds that do not require cold to germinate.

♦ Plant out wildflower plugs in meadows and long grass.

♦ Plant new wildflowers in their permanent positions in the garden.

♦ Begin mowing short lawns and paths through meadows. Summer meadow areas may be cut in March and April and then left to grow, as long as they do not contain spring flowers such as cowslips.

♦ Carefully cut any long grass areas that were left long as winter wildlife shelter, looking out for hedgehogs, voles and other small mammals. Rake off cuttings and compost them.

♦ Wildflower containers can be tidied by having last year's foliage removed. Mulch with a little fresh compost if the plants have been in the containers for some time.

♦ Sow new meadows from seed in weed free areas of soil, or sow cornfield annuals in sunny spots.

♦ Cut off last year's growth on wild climbers where necessary.

♦ Create new wildflower borders by removing turf from lawns and digging over prior to planting.

♦ Plant up new wildflower containers.

SUMMER

- In early summer cut spring meadows containing wild daffodils, cowslips, lady's smock and bugle. Allow the hay to dry and rake it off thoroughly. These areas can then be cut throughout the summer to a height of approximately 5 cms.

- In areas where the grass in new meadows is too lush and long, allow it to grow up and flower, then cut and rake in early July. Continue to cut and rake off through the summer. It may be necessary to do this for two or three years in order to reduce the soil fertility, eventually reducing the growth of the grasses.

- Continue to mow paths and short lawns. Flowery lawns can be cut fortnightly on a high cut to allow wildflowers such as clover and birds' foot trefoil to bloom.

- Top up ponds and bog gardens when the weather is dry. Use stored rainwater where possible.

- Cut down foxglove flower spikes when they have finished to encourage a further year's flowering. Make sure to save some seeds.

- Propagate aquatic wildflowers such as bogbean by uprooting small sections and planting in pots left at the water's edge.

- In late summer cut meadows and long grass to 5 cms and thoroughly rake off the hay after allowing it to dry for a day or two. Leave a few small areas uncut – these will provide winter shelter for many beneficial insects especially ladybirds and other beetles.

- Collect seeds of species you wish to propagate as they ripen. Dry well in an airing cupboard or on a windowsill out of direct sunlight, and store in paper bags or envelopes in a cool room until required for sowing.

AUTUMN

- ◆ Rake leaves from lawns and remove excess from water, but (with the exception of beech which take several years to break down) leave them to compost naturally on borders. They will add nutrients, keep in soil moisture and protect soil wildlife.

- ◆ Plant wild bulbs such as bluebells and fritillaries. Ensure they are from a reputable cultivated source and not taken from the wild.

- ◆ Remove cornfield annuals by pulling up and shaking the seeds back into the soil. Remove any perennial weeds and walk on the surface to push the seeds into the soil.

- ◆ Scatter yellow rattle seed on cut and raked meadows, especially where the soil surface is visible.

- ◆ Plant out perennial wildflowers as spaces appear in borders, or create new wildflower borders.

- ◆ Plant native climbers against walls and fences using compost and mulch where the soil is dry.

- ◆ Remove excess plant growth from ponds, disturbing wildlife as little as possible. Thin the plants in one third of the pond, thus covering the whole pond every three years.

- ◆ Continue to collect seeds of late flowering wildflowers as they ripen.

- ◆ If you grow wild grasses in borders, clumps can be split now and replanted.

- ◆ Plant native climbers and scramblers through hedges.

- ◆ In late autumn sow seeds requiring vernalisation such as cowslips, primroses, wild geraniums, hellebores and vetches. Leave pots or trays outside in a sheltered spot to allow the weather to break their dormancy.

WINTER

♦ Continue to sow wildflower seeds that require cold conditions to trigger germination (see Autumn).

♦ Plant bare-rooted wild shrubs for hedges and screens.

♦ Plan your planting for containers and window boxes.

♦ Spend the coldest days designing new borders or plant combinations.

♦ In late winter use well rotted bark to mulch around plants in dense shade, to conserve the winter's rainfall.

♦ Create a wildlife habitat in a shady place by building a log pile and adding composted bark and leaf mould.

♦ Winter is a good time to create a new pond or bog garden. Allow it to fill naturally with rainwater through the wettest months.

♦ In late winter tidy wild areas a little to encourage new growth and avoid them becoming completely overgrown. Cut back brambles and long grass in one small area each year, leaving the rest undisturbed. Over several years the whole area will be rejuvenated with minimal disturbance.

♦ In late winter or early spring, when finches have taken the seeds from old flower spikes, clip back growth on thyme, heather and other shrubby wildflowers.

89

FURTHER READING

Andrews, Jonathan, *Creating a Wild Flower Garden*, (Claremont Books 1986)

Baines, Chris, *How to Make a Wildlife Garden*, (Frances Lincoln 2000)

Blamey, Marjorie and Grey-Wilson, Christopher, *The Illustrated Flora of Britain and Northern Europe*, (Hodder and Stoughton 1989)

Gibbons, Bob and Liz, *Creating a Wildlife Garden*, (Hamlyn 1988)

Hamilton, Jill, Duchess of and Humphries, Christopher, *Native Trees and Shrubs for your Garden*, (Frances Lincoln 2005)

Kingsbury, Noel, *The Wild Flower Garden*, (Conran Octopus Limited 1994)

Lewis, Pam, *Sticky Wicket*, (Frances Lincoln 2005)

Mabey, Richard, *Flora Britannica*, (Sinclair-Stevenson 1996)

Rose, Francis, *The Wild Flower Key*, (Frederic Warne 1981)

Rose, Graham, *Woodland and Wildflower Gardening*, (David and Charles 1988)

Oudolf, Piet and Gerritsen, Henk, *Planting the Natural Garden*, (Timber Press 2003)

Robinson, William, *The Wild Garden*, (The Scolar Press 1894, reprinted 1979)

Stace, Clive, *New Flora of the British Isles*, (The Press Syndicate of the University of Cambridge 1997)

Steel, Jenny, *Meadows and Cornfields*, (Webbs Barn Designs 2001)

Steel, Jenny, *Wildflowers for Wildlife*, (Osmia Publications 2001)

Steel, Jenny, *Wildlife Ponds*, (Webbs Barn Designs 2002)

Steel, Jenny, *Butterfly Gardening*, (Webbs Barn Designs 2003)

Steel, Jenny, *Bringing a Garden to Life*, (Wiggly Wigglers 2006)

Stevens, John, *The National Trust Book of Wildflower Gardening*, (Dorling Kindersley 1987)

Warren, E. J. M., *Creating a Butterfly Garden*, (Michael Joseph 1988)

SUPPLIERS

Emorsgate Seeds, Limes Farm, Tilney All Saints, King's Lynn, Norfolk PE34 4RT
Tel. 01553 829 028 www.wildseed.co.uk Native seed of wildflowers and grasses.

Jenny Steel, The Crib, Dinchope, Craven Arms, Shropshire, SY7 9JJ
Tel. 01588 673 019 www.wildlife-gardening.co.uk Native wildflower seeds and cornfield mix.

National Wildflower Centre, Court Hey Park, Roby Road, Liverpool, L16 3NA
Tel. 0151 738 1913 www.wildflower.org.uk Wildflower plants and seeds.

Naturescape, Maple Farm, Coach Gap Lane, Langar, Nottingham, NG13 9HP
Tel. 01949 860 592 www.naturescape.co.uk Wildflower plants, bulbs and seeds.

Natural Surroundings, Centre for Wildlife Gardening and Conservation, Bayfield Estate, Holt, Norfolk NR25 7JN
Tel. 01263 711 091 www.naturalsurroundings.org.uk Wildflower plants, bulbs and seeds.

John Shipton, Y Felin, Henllan Amgoed, Whitland, Carmarthenshire , SA34 0SL
Tel. 01994 240 125 www.bluebellbulbs.co.uk Native bulbs and ferns.

Wiggly Wigglers, Lower Blakemere Farm, Blakemere, Hereford, HR2 9PX
Tel. 01981 500 391 www.wigglywigglers.co.uk Wildflower plants, plugs and seeds.

ORGANISATIONS

Botanical Society of the British Isles, Botany Department, The Natural History Museum, Cromwell Road, London, SW7 5BD www.bsbi.org.uk

Butterfly Conservation, Manor Yard, East Lulworth, Wareham, Dorset, BH20 5QP
Tel. 0870 774 4309 www.butterfly-conservation.org

Flora Locale, Denford Manor, Hungerford, Berkshire, RG7 0UN
Tel. 01488 680 457 www.floralocale.org

Natural England, Northminster House, Peterborough PE1 1UA
Tel. 0845 600 3078 www.naturalengland.org.uk

Plantlife, 14 Rollestone Street, Salisbury, Wiltshire, SP1 1DX
Tel 01722 342 730 www.plantlife.org.uk

The Wildlife Trusts, The Kiln, Waterside, Mather Road, Newark, Nottinghamshire, NG24 1WT
Tel. 0870 036 7711 www.wildlifetrusts.org

INDEX

About the author

Jenny Steel grew up in the middle of Oxford, where as a child she counted the ladybirds in her mother's organic garden and watched the many swifts that flew overhead. Her passion for wildlife and the outdoors led to a Master's Degree at Oxford University in Plant Ecology and research on topics including pollination, nutrient recycling in woodland and a study of arable weeds. In 1990 she established a plant nursery in Oxfordshire growing and supplying wildflowers to the increasing numbers of wildlife gardeners. She now concentrates on writing books, and contributes to magazines and a variety of websites. She also teaches wildlife gardening and wildflower gardening courses. She has worked with many companies and organisations including English Nature, the RHS, Usborne Books, the organic gardening company Wiggly Wigglers, Oxfordshire County Council, the Snowdonia National Park Study Centre and several of the Wildlife Trusts.

She now lives in South Shropshire where she and her husband are creating a new wildlife garden. Jenny has written five other books on wildlife and wildflower gardening, loves birdwatching and walking in wild places, and has a passion for wildflower meadows.